THE SPIRIT OF ELIJAH
GOD'S END TIME MOVE

THE SPIRIT OF ELIJAH
GOD'S END TIME MOVE

By
Dr. Sherlock Bally

Published by:
Susan K. Reidel
Logos to Rhema Publishing
sreidel@hotmail.com
(918) 606-5346

Unless otherwise noted, all Scripture taken from

THE KING JAMES VERSION

ISBN -10#
ISBN -13#

*Published in the
United States of America by*

Susan K. Reidel
Logos to Rhema Publishing
sreidel@hotmail.com
(918) 606-5346

Printed in the United States of America

Dedication

There are not very many times in ministry when you meet a servant of God with prophetic insight, tempered with a holy balance and a compassion for people. When you meet such a person, it is a wonderful moment.

Pastor Ronnie Pittman of Glory Tabernacle in Ashville, NC is one of those rare and humble men who has eternity in his heart.

I dedicate this book to him because of an experience I had in his office and the inspiration that was multiplied in me because of his words that were sharp, precise, and prophetic. I bless you my brother.

From the bottom of my heart, Thank You!!

CONTENTS

Introduction

There is a great expectation in many believers that a genuine move of God will take place before the rapture of the church. I am one of those believers. So an equally great question emerges. What will be the nature of this move of God? Will it look like anything that went before us?

There were significant moves of God all through history that produced a spiritual shaking in our world. I believe that the Bible gives great insight as to what this end-time move will be and also shows what it will produce.

This particular book has been incubating in my inner man for many years and I now feel released by the Almighty God to write it. As you read this, let your heart not be closed by opinions and ideas from the past. I know that many are hungering for the supernatural touch of God and are wanting to be used by God in these days of enormous challenge. As we move together through these pages, may the presence of this move of God, the nature of this move become a reality to you.

Chapter 1

The Move of God
or
The Mayhem of Satan

There is disagreement within Christian circles concerning what will happen in the church before the rapture of the church. There is a significant segment of the Christian movement that believes that the church will be fragmented, visionless, meandering and purposeless at the time of the rapture. They believe that there will be and that there actually is a severe and serious apostasy or departure from the faith that will characterize the church before the rapture. Many see no evidence or have no hope for a move of God before the church is taken away by rapture. They are adamant in their position because their response is, *"I see no evidence of the move of God in the church."* So by saying this, they relegate the move of God to a place of non-existence or irrelevance. They are saying that the church will have no power or message to be preached as a witness to the on-looking world. They look at many Christians who are consumed by the cares of life, swallowed by the seductions of the world and immobilized by materialism and they see no hope for the move of God. I personally know many teachers and preachers of reputation that hold this view. Even in the circles of Bible Prophecy where there is teaching about the coming of the Lord, many teach this as the reality.

All of this belief comes because of what is evident within the realm of church life. I cannot contest the fact that there are many whose priorities are completely reversed neither can I disagree with the fact that materialism and humanism have assumed a fairly prominent position in church life. How sad that stressing the material and stressing the rights of the individual have assumed a position in church life. Here the emphasis should be spiritual and the rights of God should be pre-eminent.

I cannot disagree with the fact that some have departed from the faith.

1 Timothy 4:1&2 states: *"¹Now the Spirit speaketh expressly, that in the latter times some*

shall depart from the faith, giving heed to seducing spirits, and doctrines of devils; 2 Speaking lies in hypocrisy; having their conscience seared with a hot iron;"

Think about this for one moment. Some have departed from the faith which means that they were in the faith. They have given heed to seducing spirits because when you leave the realm of the Holy Spirit, you will enter another realm. They now give heed to doctrines of devils because when you have purposely departed from true doctrine, you will be engulfed by satanic doctrine. The purpose of the enemy causing departure from God's Word, from true doctrine, is to get men and women consumed by false doctrine or doctrines of devils. This is the path to delusion and destruction.

And this is a cardinal mistake. We must never forget that the many have never decided the move of God. The destiny of the church is never decided by the support of the majority. In most cases the majority are not interested in adhering to true doctrine and spiritual commitment. It seems as though the majority find the path of least resistance and frame their own realities by adjusting the word of God instead of adjusting their lives. The doctrines of devils will provide a path of ease and convenience but lead to deception, destruction and devastation. This is the ultimate aim of the enemy.

The reason that the devil has brought these doctrines of devils to such a place of deception is clear. Only spiritual deception can cause people to walk this path to their own destruction. It is more than a societal problem, or an economic problem, or a political problem, it is spiritual deception. This is the worst of them all.

FROM THE FEW TO THE MANY

Almighty God has always had a witness, a few, a remnant, a people that He has raised and restored, that have brought a message that affected the world. It was Moses, then Joshua to Caleb, then the 70 that led an entire nation. It was Elijah, then the 7000 that touched a nation. It was Gideon and the three hundred that delivered a nation. It was Esther and Mordecai that turned back the plot of Haman and a nation was saved. When Athaliah destroyed all the royal seed it was a child, Joash who was hidden, and he began to reign at 7 years old bringing great revival to the land. When the land seems to be overrun with false prophecies, when the flame of the witness is flickering, when it seems as though the zero hour is here, GOD ALWAYS HAS A PEOPLE. In the case of Joash, he was hidden, in the case of the 7000 in Elijah's day, they were hidden, but in the moment of spiritual desperation they were called forth. Jesus chose 12 men from obscurity and from these twelve, He shook a world.

Here is the central truth and the fundamental point that is not considered. God works from the few to the many, from the in to the out, from the darkness to the light and from death to life. All through the record of Holy Scripture, Almighty God has had a people, who would take a stand for Him. They began as few in number but because of His power and their obedience, the numbers dramatically increased as others were touched.

It is here that I have a different view from many others. I believe that the Almighty will always have a witness of Himself and when it seems that places are overrun with false witnesses, God's remnant, God's few will rise in power. Those who would define the pre-rapture times by looking at the behavior of the many are overlooking the power of God to raise a few.

LOSING POWER
OVER THE FURNACE

I believe the book of Daniel is one of the most relevant books today. It deals with the chosen people in bondage to a king, with delusions of godhood that wants to be worshipped. Here a vicious attack is leveled on those who would not bow to the image that was created. The purpose of this image was to command the worship of God's people to be directed to the king and a furnace was prepared to incinerate those who would not bow to this image. In fact, the furnace was heated 7 times hotter and then Shadrach, Meshach and Abednego were thrown into the furnace.

In all of Babylon, in the midst of this haughty king and rebellious empire, God had a few, who were then taken and thrown into a furnace where several miracles happened. One of these miracles was that a fourth man showed up who had power over the furnace. When this fourth man stepped in, the king lost power over the furnace he had commanded to be built. Having lost power over his furnace, his purposes for the furnace were obviously annulled.

Daniel 3:26-30 states: "*²⁶Then Nebuchadnezzar came near to the mouth of the burning fiery furnace, and spake, and said, Shadrach, Meshach, and Abednego, ye servants of the most high God, come forth, and come hither. Then Shadrach, Meshach, and Abednego, came forth of the midst of the fire. ²⁷And the princes, governors, and captains, and the king's counsellors, being gathered together, saw these men, upon whose bodies the fire had no power, nor was a hair of their head singed, neither were their coats changed, nor the smell of fire had passed on them. ²⁸Then Nebuchadnezzar spake, and said, Blessed be the God of Shadrach, Meshach, and Abednego, who hath sent his angel, and delivered his servants that trusted in him, and have changed the king's word, and yielded their bodies, that they might not serve nor worship any god, except their own God. ²⁹ Therefore I make a decree, That every people, nation, and language, which speak anything amiss against the God of Shadrach, Meshach, and Abednego, shall be cut in pieces, and their houses shall be made a dunghill: because there is no other God that can deliver after this sort. ³⁰ Then the king promoted*

Shadrach, Meshach, and Abednego, in the province of Babylon."

What a testimony from a furnace through a few. The mighty king had to recognize the Mightiest King. He said, *'Ye servants of the MOST HIGH GOD.'* Then he said, *'Blessed be the God of Shadrach, Meshach and Abednego.'* Then he said *'Their God changed the King's WORD';* then he made a decree that if anyone said anything against the God of these men, they would be cut into pieces. He said, *'There is no other God like this.'* and the result was that these three were promoted in Babylon.

God wanted His men promoted in the midst of Babylon, in the midst of false worship, where a king with an anti-christ spirit ruled, in a place where an image was built to command worship. It was here, where the majority were bowing, surrendering, that a few stood. For a time, the entire country knew of the glorious God of these three young men and the king had to realize the sovereignty, the supremacy, and the superiority of our GOD.

God has never needed the numeric majority to do what He has chosen to do. There are a few, there is a remnant, a group of people in the church that are contending for the move of God. I see this as I travel around the country and the world.

THE TWO CAMPS

Yes there are two camps in the church today, one that is defecting from the faith, departing from the power and living a surface, superficial life. But there is another camp that is expecting the move of God, that will do all it takes to see this happen. They have a heart to see the world impacted for the glory of God. There is a camp of apostasy but there is also the camp of revival. This is dramatically seen in the book of Revelation 3, where two camps with different beliefs, different doctrines, and different destinies emerge.

Let me approach this firstly from the perspective of Revelation 3:14-22 which states: *"14 And unto the angel of the church of the Laodiceans write; These things saith the Amen, the faithful and true witness, the beginning of the creation of God; 15 I know thy works, that thou art neither cold nor hot: I would thou wert cold or hot. 16 So then because thou art lukewarm, and neither cold nor hot, I will spue thee out of my mouth. 17 Because thou sayest, I am rich, and increased with goods, and have need of nothing; and knowest not that thou art wretched, and miserable, and poor, and blind, and naked: [18] I counsel thee to buy of me gold tried in the fire, that thou mayest be rich; and white raiment, that thou mayest be clothed, and that the shame of thy nakedness do not appear; and anoint thine eyes with eyesalve, that thou mayest see. [19] As many as I love, I rebuke and chasten: be zealous therefore, and repent. [20] Behold, I stand at the door, and knock: if any man hear my voice, and open the door, I will come in to him, and will sup with him, and he with me. [21] To him that overcometh will I grant to sit with me in my throne, even as I also overcame, and am set down with my Father in his throne. [22] He that hath an ear, let him hear what the Spirit saith unto the churches."*

I have quoted these scriptures so that it would be right before you and highly visible. This book is not meant to be a treatment on the churches of the Revelation but to illustrate the point of the two camps, and I am compelled to give a limited treatment to two of these churches.

To the church of Laodicea, Jesus is known as the Amen, the faithful and true witness. This indicates that this church needed the true doctrine, the true word and they needed to see Jesus as King and the final word. This also indicates conversely that this church would be dealing with false doctrine and they therefore needed the authority of His Word. He is also called in this scripture, "the beginning or the creation of God." As the firstborn of God, He must be heeded and obeyed because all that was to come was because of Him. He must have preeminence in His church. Almighty God declares that because this church is neither that, because this church is neither hot nor cold but they are lukewarm, He will spew them out of His mouth.

They held the position of apathy, indifference and lethargy. They were neither hot, on fire for God nor cold, rejection of God. They occupied that faded, jaded territory where their hypocrisy thrived. This caused God to vomit them out, and I would say, straight into the tribulation period. A life that is lived in the twilight where there is neither light not darkness is a life that is irrelevant and anemic. These are the ones who are present but have little or no impact. These lives are woven in the web of convenience and personal preference. The drive is to survive and they possess little or no passion to pursue the things of God.

Their grasp is of the present because the future has little value to them. It is the life of satisfying the present appetites and so the power of the spiritual birthright is secondary. They are reprints and replicas of Esau where a pot of beans is the preference to the spiritual birthright. The satisfaction of present appetites is more important than God's plan. Their grasp for the present has eliminated their reach for the future. They are quite content to be absorbed by the cares of life and to have spiritual priorities eroded. The physical takes precedence over the spiritual, the present over the future, the grasp over the reach, and the cares of life over the things of God. Here they live, in a spiritual dead sea, in the doldrums of apathy, with waning of strength, and compromised commitment. They possess a profession of God but not a commitment to Him. There is rhetorical talk but no purposeful walk. There is a boast of information but no evidence of transformation. There is a form of godliness but no force of His power against sin.

We must answer this question. How many in church life does this describe? You may ask "Why spend the time identifying these elements?" I must tell you that it is a powerful thing, as a child of God and a servant of God to see these elements and attitudes in church life. We all deal with this wrestling, with the struggles, with the challenges of spiritual life. But, we must not be lost in a maze of activity without seeing and knowing who we are, without the development of spiritual character.

There is a vivid illustration of this in 1 Samuel12:1-12 "*1 And the LORD sent Nathan unto David. And he came unto him, and said unto him, There were two men in one city; the one rich, and the other poor. 2 The rich man had exceeding many flocks and herds: 3But the poor man had nothing, save one little ewe lamb, which he had bought and nourished up: and it grew up together with him, and with his children; it did eat of his own meat, and drank of his own cup, and lay in his bosom, and was unto him as a daughter. 4And there came a traveler unto the rich man, and he spared to take of his own flock and of his own herd, to dress for the wayfaring man that was come unto him; but took the poor man's lamb, and dressed it for the man that was come to him. 5And David's anger was greatly kindled against the man; and he said to Nathan, As the LORD liveth, the man that hath done this thing shall surely die: ⁶And he shall restore the lamb fourfold, because he did this thing, and because he had no pity. ⁷And Nathan said to David, Thou art the man. Thus saith the LORD God of Israel, I anointed thee king over Israel, and I delivered thee out of the hand of Saul; ⁸And I gave thee thy master's house, and thy master's wives into thy bosom, and gave thee the house of Israel and of Judah; and if that had been too little, I would moreover have given unto thee such and such things. ⁹Wherefore hast thou despised the commandment of the LORD, to do evil in his sight? thou hast killed Uriah the Hittite with the sword, and hast taken his wife to be thy wife, and hast slain him with the sword of the children of Ammon. ¹⁰Now therefore the sword shall never depart from thine house; because thou hast despised me, and hast taken the wife of Uriah the Hittite to be thy wife. ¹¹Thus saith the LORD, Behold, I will raise up evil against thee out of thine own house, and I will take thy wives before thine eyes, and give them unto thy neighbor, and he shall lie with thy wives in the sight of this sun. ¹²For thou didst it secretly: but I will do this thing before all Israel, and before the sun."*

Nathan the prophet comes to David with a prophetic word from the Almighty God that was specifically for King David. There were two men in one city, one was very rich, the other very poor. The rich man had many flocks of sheep and herds of cattle and the poor man had one lamb. The poor man reared this lamb with his children and this animal grew up within this poor family. A traveler came to the rich man and instead of taking one of his many animals to kill to feed the traveler, he took the one lamb of the poor man and killed it.

When King David heard this word, he was incensed and angered. He then asked Nathan to tell him who had done such a thing because he would surely die. He continued that there would be restoration to the poor man four-fold because of what was taken from him. Then Nathan brought the stunning news to King David, "The man is you." David had been anointed king and he was delivered out of the hands of Saul. He was given his master's house, his master's wives and the house of Israel and Judah. But he despised the commandment of God and did evil in God's sight and killed Uriah. He then took Uriah's wife, even though David had many of his own wives. Now there would be evil in his house and God would take his wives before his eyes and give them unto his neighbor.

There are some astonishing issues in this prophetic word. King David, with all the promise, the victories, with all the extensions of the Kingdom that he was used to taking, fell into this trap. His career was magnificent but there came a point when his character suffered grievously. You must not get to the place where your accomplishments, your success, your possessions bring you to the place where the extent of your spiritual commitment is unimportant. You cannot get to the place where spiritual character is unimportant because of the things you hold in your hand.

David did not know that the prophet was speaking to him. His ears were shut to the word of the Lord and his eyes were blinded to the word of the Lord. He could not hear and could not see. The sounds of accomplishment were so loud that he could not hear the word of the Lord. The wealth he saw was so glorious, he could not see the direction he was going. Wow! What a tragedy to happen to a man of such calling, such calling, such anointing, such purpose. He could not see the relevance of this prophecy to taking the one husband of Bathseba, when he, the King, had so many. King David's anger was kindled against the rich man that took the one lamb but never saw the parallel to his life and his situation and his actions.

How many times have special people, people with special callings fallen into the trap where no word, no vision is relevant to their situation and actions. Its application, its relevance is someone else, when the intention of God is to speak to the individual. David was blinded in plain sight, he was immobilized in the midst of great activity. He got to the deepest depth of depravity because he looked to the highest point of personal accomplishment. Whether he felt justified because of his position, whether he felt deserving because of his power, his sin trapped him. I have spent these painful moments, to remind you that character must come before career, your walk must come before your talk, and your profession must come before your possession. May we not be blinded, deceived, seduced, but may we stand and say to our Father, "Here am I, help me."

THIS CHURCH'S OPINION OF ITSELF

Verse 17 of Revelation 3 begins with the word "because" so is linked to verse 16. The reason for this lukewarm condition is given in verse 17 and it is extremely revealing. Verse 17 says, *"Because you say*

I am rich, I am increased with goods and I have need of nothing." This is the nature of the church that characterizes the spirit of the age. Several things become very apparent concerning this camp in the scripture. There is a pre-occupation with 'I' and an absorption with material things, so humanism and materialism are the essential qualities of this church. Remember, it is the church of Laodicea. It is obvious that God is not offended by riches or goods because He is Lord above it all. It is not whether you have things, it is whether things have you.

Yet I find a deeply disturbing thought in this verse. I reiterate, it is not the possession of things that is offensive to the Almighty God. It is clear in scripture that it is the will of God for His people to prosper and be in health as their soul prospers. It is not the fact that they were rich that brought this immediate indictment of God. It was the attitude of, *"I AM"*. The Almighty God is the only I AM. Here in this church of Laodicea, the attitude of the people was not just the profession of the wealth but the utter displacement of God and the replacement of God by themselves. They were adopting the attitude of superiority and supremacy. These words I AM rich, with the emphasis of I AM spoke of a sinister idolatry that was taking place in the church. It was not gods of stone and clay that men bowed to, but they bowed to the idol of self in the church. This is the attitude that the antichrist will represent as he endeavors to deceive the world. The word 'anti' does not just mean against but it also means instead of. This attitude in Laodicea is an attitude that is the most dangerous.

There is no company more dangerous to keep, than the company of the antichrist and the spirit of the antichrist. Follow the degenerative sequence of events. First this church does everything according to its own will. So beware of the attitude that says I will do what I want, when I want, how I want. This church exalts itself so beware of the attitude of superiority and self-promotion. It magnifies itself so beware of the attitude that exhibits the, 'I must be seen,' lifestyle. It speaks against God so beware of the subtlety of speaking for and of yourself and against the will of God. This is stuff that you would never dream could be a part of church life or even more dangerously, a dominant part of church life.

So God's response to their profession of being rich, and increased with goods having need of nothing was and is, that they were wretched, miserable, poor, blind and naked. It is still fairly overwhelming to think that people who are involved in church life can say, *"I have need of nothing."* This is the depth that the pursuit of the rights of the individual will take you to -complete independence from God. This kind of attitude, lifestyle represents one camp in the realm of church life. However, thanks be to God, there is another camp.

THE CHURCH OF PHILADELPHIA

Revelation 3:7-12 states: *"⁷And to the angel of the church in Philadelphia write; These things saith he that is holy, he that is true, he that hath the key of David, he that openeth, and no man shutteth; and shutteth, and no man openeth; ⁸I know thy works: behold, I have set before thee an open door, and no man can shut it: for thou hast a little strength, and hast kept my word, and hast not denied my name. ⁹Behold, I will make them of the synagogue of Satan, which say they are Jews, and are not, but do lie; behold, I will make them to come and worship before thy feet, and to know that I have loved thee. ¹⁰Because thou hast kept the word of my patience, I also will keep thee from the hour of temptation, which shall come upon all the world, to try them that dwell upon the earth. ¹¹Behold, I come quickly: hold that fast which thou hast, that no man take thy crown.*

12Him that overcometh will I make a pillar in the temple of my God, and he shall go no more out: and I will write upon him the name of my God, and the name of the city of my God, which is new Jerusalem, which cometh down out of heaven from my God: and I will write upon him my new name."

The character of Jesus visible in this church is amazing and powerful and very indicative of the plan of God before the rapture of the church. When men say that they only see apostasy, departure, deflection, seduction in the church and they cannot see the hope or the move of God, this text must be read. Jesus is described here as He who is holy and He who is true. Holiness and truth will be the marks of this church. One brings internal deliverance the other external deliverance. They are given the key of DAVID which means the key of the household and signifies the key of supply. A door is opened before then and I submit to you that this is the door of harvest. There is also a shut door and I submit to you that as the door of the systems of the world are being shut, the door of harvest is being opened. This church has a little strength but has not denied His name. They have stood, represented, reached and preached.

Verse 10 says that God will keep them from the hour of temptation which shall come upon the world. No form of tribulation has come upon the entire world but there is a tribulation period coming and this church will be taken out of it. Here is a church experiencing the move of holiness and truth, with an open door to harvest. They have a little strength, have kept His word and not denied his name. This is by no means a perfect church, but it is a committed church, that is obedient, and has the harvest in its heart. There is a church that some see and the church that God sees. With God, it has always been the few, the remnant whereas, with people, it has always been the numeric majority.

I had to present these thoughts at the beginning of this book so that you could see the two camps in the church. When I say the church in this context, I mean the church you see, or the institutional church. There are people, be they few, whose hearts are still filled with eternity, whose lives are committed to God. There are people where the vision is God's vision and where dreams are about all that God wants. I have personal relationship and fellowship with some of these people. I am honored to have them in my circle and I am all the better for knowing them. I have two friends who have stood with me unconditionally whose name I will not mention. I must add that my dear wife, Renee, has been my support and has stood with me for 39 years. She has paid a dear price for having me gone as many weeks out of the year as I am and has remained committed and loving. I love her dearly. My son and daughter have been a blessing to me and I am very thankful for their lives.

Apart from my family, I am connected to so many, so many that I consider to be remnant believers, Philadelphian believers who are ready to do whatever is required. There are many pastors in this country that are contending for the move of God and I am personally acquainted with scores of them. There are many of the younger generation that have adopted a bit of a different approach to ministry. They are being used of the Lord and many of the churches they are pastoring are growing dramatically. Some of these younger pastors are sons of more traditional pastors and are being used of the Lord in a wonderful way.

One of the things that have been a refreshing breeze to me, is what I have seen in many of these pastors in their 30s and 40s. Many of them have developed a passion for the presence of God but with a difference. Their approach, their methodology are strikingly different from what would be considered the norm, but they have remained focused on pursuing the presence of God. I know some of those that are in Frankfort Ky, Rockport Tx, Festus Missouri, Five Rivers Trinidad and many others. Some of these pastors are pastoring churches of 1400 people. I must say to you, that I have been so blessed to see, with their success, with their approval, this overriding priority of, for the presence of the Almighty God. I see this move, I see men and women emerging as modern day Elijahs with all the use of modern day technology, with all the difference, the method, the move of God remains at the ""Epicenter." HALLELUJAH!!!

I spoke of the younger generation of pastors who have refused to make the presence of God secondary to methods and approaches in ministry. In this society of the microwave moments, do it now, commuter and computer, these men are to be commended for contending for the move of God.

But it would be inappropriate for me not to speak about the pastors of more mature age and experience. These are the men that have blazed the trail and still are and have prepared the way for the emerging ministries. I have seen in many of these, the passion for the presence of God. The length of years in ministry has not diminished their passion for the presence of God. I personally know many of these precious servants of God. One of them as of this writing is a Bishop in South West Texas. He called me and asked me to be the keynote speaker at his camp meeting where several churches and their pastors and leaders would be in attendance. As my normal practice is, I asked him, what he would like my emphasis to be. He said, in the morning sessions he wanted me to speak on Bible Prophecy and the nation of Israel. His next statement was one of great significance. He then said, "I want the presence of God in the night meetings in a supernatural way. I want to see my leaders touched, restored, challenged and set on fire by the power of the Holy Spirit."

I was deeply touched and moved because one of the greatest revelations God has given me is on "The Glory of God". As of this date, I have written two books on Glory. The first is called *Glory, Where Atmospheres Collide* and the second *Walking in God's Glory Realm*. I am writing a third on Glory called, *God's Glory, God's Order, Not Your Way*. When the bishop said this, I immediately knew that this was a man of special heart and caliber. I say to you, Bishop Bob Jayne, you are a part of a special move of God before the coming of the Messiah. In that camp meeting there was a special sovereign move of God where people, where pastors and leaders were touched by the Almighty God. Some of the testimonies were astounding.

Yes, God has His men and women, of all ages, many with different methods, different approaches. But one thing remains consistent, they all want, hunger for and are passionate for His presence. Choose you this day whom you will serve. Choose you this day, to which camp you determine to belong. Remember, you can spend your life anyway you choose, but you only get to spend it once. Spend it well my friend, spend it well.

Chapter 2

What is The Spirit of Elijah?

Malachi 4:5,6: "⁵ Behold, I will send you Elijah the prophet before the coming of the great and dreadful day of the LORD: ⁶And he shall turn the heart of the fathers to the children, and the heart of the children to their fathers, lest I come and smite the earth with a curse."

Luke 1:17: "¹⁷And he shall go before him in the spirit and power of Elias, to turn the hearts of the fathers to the children, and the disobedient to the wisdom of the just; to make ready a people prepared for the Lord."

Mark 9:12: "¹² And he answered and told them, Elias verily cometh first, and restoreth all things; and how it is written of the Son of man, that he must suffer many things, and be set at nought."

When you consider these verses in harmony with one another, the revelation on the move of God in the end-time is clear. God said in Malachi 4:1 that He would send Elijah before the great and dreadful day of the Lord. He will be sent into the tribulation period before the battle of Armageddon as one of the two witnesses. This lets you know even in a time of extreme tribulation, when the Spirit of God is lifted as the barrier to evil and the full gamut of evil is revealed, God still has a witness. It is ludicrous to think that God will ensure He has a witness in the tribulation, in Elijah, in the angels preaching the gospel of the Kingdom, in the 144,000 and the other witnesses and he be without a witness today. That deception or seduction will be so prolific that there will be no witness of His power and might, is un-thinkable. So let us examine the Spirit of Elijah.

The spirit of Elijah by definition has to do with Elijah and I will explain the vital connection. How-ever, before I do this, we must understand Elijah and what he was called to do. In the tribulation period, we know he comes and stands against the power of the antichrist. The Antichrist claims to be God so Elijah vehemently stands against this claim. The Antichrist through the false prophet will institute the mark of the beast so that people can be controlled but also it becomes a form of worship. The Antichrist will launch a hateful campaign against Israel but Elijah will be a stalwart for his people. He will be used to manifest the supernatural power of Almighty God. The miracles that will be used to reveal God's power in the Tribulation period bear an exact similarity to what Elijah did in the Old Testament. The two witnesses in the Tribulation period, one of whom is Elijah, cannot be touched until the time of their testimony is finished. Again, they are not able to be touched until the time of their testimony is finished.

So think on the prophetic parallel for a few moments. The Antichrist today is not yet physically revealed.

But, 1 John 4:1-6 states: *"Beloved, believe not every spirit, but try the spirits whether they are of God: because many false prophets are gone out into the world. ² Hereby know ye the Spirit of God: Every spirit that confesseth that Jesus Christ is come in the flesh is of God: ³ And every spirit that confesseth not that Jesus Christ is come in the flesh is not of God: and this is that spirit of antichrist, whereof ye have heard that it should come; and even now already is it in the world. [4] Ye are of God, little children, and have overcome them: because greater is he that is in you, than he that is in the world. [5] They are of the world: therefore speak they of the world, and the world heareth them. [6] We are of God: he that knoweth God heareth us; he that is not of God heareth not us. Hereby know we the spirit of truth, and the spirit of error."*

THE SPIRIT OF ANTICHRIST

We know that the spirit of the Antichrist is all over the world and this spirit is given detailed treatment in the word of God. We are called to stand against the power of the spirit of the Antichrist. We quote the Scripture hundreds of times. *"Greater is He that is in you than he that is in the world,"* but many never examine the context. The context of this Scripture is concerning He that is in you, the Holy Spirit, who is greater than he that is in the world, the spirit of the Antichrist.

The battle is essentially spirit versus spirit. Elijah will stand against the claim that the antichrist is God. We must point out that the presence of all these little new age gods is evidence of the spirit of the antichrist that is in the world today. The purpose of this spirit of the antichrist is three fold. It is to make the abnormal seem normal so when the abnormal claims of the antichrist are made they will be readily accepted. It is to introduce a worldly scale of values so that life will not be defined by the value system of the word of God. It is to desensitize people to the realm of evil so that evil will be accepted or even preferred.

We stand against the puny idols of humanism, materialism, secularism, and 'meism'. We break every idol that will endeavor to steal the worship of the believer.

As the Antichrist initiates a campaign against Israel in the tribulation period so too we see the spirit of the antichrist fomenting hatred against the land of Israel, the people of Israel and the holy city of Jerusalem. The church must take a stand in prayer, must take a moral stand against this spirit. It is noticeable, though, that such a stand for Israel is becoming increasingly unpopular, even in church realms.

Elijah was used mightily in the realm of the supernatural so that there was a visible witness of

God's power. So too, in these moments of time, we must believe that Almighty God can do it again through His people. The two witnesses, during the Tribulation, are not able to be touched until the time of their testimony is finished. This is the faith and confidence that we all must flow in. As long as we are following the commission of our Lord, and He is leading us, no enemy, power or force has the power to terminate us.

ELIJAH'S SUDDEN EMERGENCE

So we return to Elijah who suddenly emerges on Israel's scene in a time of extreme crisis. Jezebel is on a Satanic rampage as she destroys the altars of the Almighty God. She installs her evil monstrous gods and institutes a depth of evil that was hitherto unknown. Add to this the shameful backsliding of a nation and the treacherous acts of her gullible, weak, puppet husband. The state religion was the worship of Baal and Asherah and at this point when crisis appears in every sector of this empire, a prophet emerges.

He stands in opposition to this empire, challenging the entire realm of idolatry. When he sees this damnable priesthood, with liquid fire in his voice, he declares that he will not be quiet. Even being chased by Jezebel, at the mouth of the cave, he makes a statement that will never be forgotten;

> 1 Kings 19:10, 14 states: *"¹¹And he said, Go forth, and stand upon the mount before the LORD. And, behold, the LORD passed by, and a great and strong wind rent the mountains, and brake in pieces the rocks before the LORD; but the LORD was not in the wind: and after the wind an earthquake; but the LORD was not in the earthquake: ¹⁴And he said, I have been very jealous for the LORD God of hosts: because the children of Israel have forsaken thy covenant, thrown down thine altars, and slain thy prophets with the sword; and I, even I only, am left; and they seek my life, to take it away."*

He declares a jealousy for the honor of the Almighty God and he expresses an opposition to this idolatry that is unparalleled. Yes, jealousy in defense of the divine honor of the Lord. Yes, Elijah, from the mountains, Yes, Elijah the Tishbite, he stands with unflagging faith and unflinching courage. His heart burns with the flames of 1,000 furnaces, it burns with righteous anger and indignation at the attitude of accommodation and surrender to the puny gods of these idolaters. He has a holy passion to adhere to obey and declare the word of the Almighty God. No threat, no human authority, no king or queen can cause him to deny his call or to be deterred from his mission.

Elijah is called the prophet of deeds and Moses is called the prophet of the law. This is a man that authored no script, gave no Old Testament books but demonstrated the power of God like no other. Yes! When the zero hour has come, when the valleys are filled and the mountains are overrun with corruption, Elijah emerges. When even God's people seem, to have their lives reduced, when their lamps of witness are flickering to an inch of being extinguished, here in this crisis moment God raises His Elijah.

THE PARALLEL TODAY

So too today, it seems as though human authority has done all it can to institute the idolatry of humanism and materialism. In this time, leaders have become antagonistic to God, to His Son Jesus, and to the church of the Almighty. Today, many Christians, to a great degree have sacrificed their passion and their commitment on the altars of ease and compromise. But today, Almighty God is staging, once again, His powerful intervention. He is raising men and women with a holy jealousy in their hearts for the honor of God. Would to God that men and women arise to take the position of holy jealousy, righteous indignation, Godly anger against idolatry. It is not only that a king and queen would build temples to false gods and erect idols. It is that the people of God, the people of Israel would surrender to these pagan gods, and bow in worship to these hand made gods. They would descend to the depths of this heathenism and forsake the worship of the true God. Elijah rose with a no compromise, no accommodation, fearless attitude and a thunderous message. Where are these men and women today who will announce that this idolatry is not acceptable and it will be judged, and the judgment begins today? To think of where Elijah has come from, where he is now, to whom he is speaking and what he is saying, lets you know the miracle of this moment as he faces squarely, the evil of his day.

THE TURNING POINTS

It is again of vital importance to understand the character of Elijah, the process he went through, the extent of his mission because it all forms a prophetic pattern. Malachi 4:6 begins with, *"He shall turn the hearts,"* so his was a mission of turning hearts. The mission was related to fathers and children. He will turn the hearts of the fathers to the children and children to the fathers. Think about the impact on the entire world if children and fathers were in the proper relationship. What percentage of the trauma of our society would be eliminated if fathers and children were in right standing? So included in this mission of Elijah are turning points in families.

I would like to present a thought on this familial restoration. We know that when Elijah comes during the tribulation period, he will turn hearts of the people of Israel to the Father, to Almighty God. Think about God the Father turning His heart to His people and His people turning their hearts to the Father. Then think of the spiritual Father in the church, the pastor turning his heart to the children and then the church people turning their hearts to the spiritual father.

Think of the tremendous impact of these three operations in relation to fathers and children. Family units are being devastated by the absence of fatherly love and guidance. Children emerge with rebellion, and chaos because of the lack of fatherly authority and guidance. Look at the hopelessness of so many of your generation and much of it can be attributed to fatherless homes. I find it fascinating that 2,500 years ago the state of today's world was revealed.

Today, young men and women are strewn on the rocks of fatherless homes. Single mothers are now very common, the single parent homes have become a part of society. The family unit has been beaten and battered and this attack has caused a great disintegration. The spirit of Elijah, this prophetic move, Thank God, has to do with the revival and restoration of the family.

Look at the condition of church life in general and see the lack of submission to pastoral authority and the lack of true discipleship in the church. This has led, generally speaking, to a church where people are absorbed by other interests and have not fulfilled the great commission. Most of the Christians of today have never won a soul and have no interest in being involved in personal evangelism. There is none or very little impartation from pastor to people so there is very little multiplication of disciples in the house of God. Once again, the great problem here is solved when the spiritual father turns his heart to the children, then the children turn their hearts to the spiritual father. Think of what will happen when Almighty God turns His heart to Israel and then Israel turns its heart to the Father. Yes, their ultimate Yom Kippur, the Day of Atonement would arrive. The mission of Elijah to turn the hearts of the Father to children and children to the fathers will bring a restoration or a move of God in a way that is revolutionary.

FATHERS AND SONS

Malachi 4:6 states that if Elijah does not come and turn the hearts then God will smite the earth with a curse. The astonishing indication is clear and that is if there is not a move with fathers and children, a curse will come upon the earth. The attack of the devil on fatherhood is now unveiled as a major strategy to destroy the entire fabric of society. Societal chaos can be traced to these tremendous attacks on fatherhood. If there is no fatherhood then there would be no sonship. The Scripture declares that you have many instructors but few fathers. Instructors will give you matters of information, fathers will give formation. I know that many have stereotyped the move of God and made it predictable but the greatest need today remains the need for fathers to assume their God-given position.

This prophetic move, this spirit of Elijah move of God will touch the hearts of fathers and sons. When others are looking for a replay of the move of God as it was in the past years, this present, different move, this restoration is one that is of vital relevance to our lives today.

KING OF HEARTS

The Scripture teaching that this end-time move has to do with families, whether it is the family of God, the family unit, or the church family is amazing. One of the things that are overlooked is that this involves the turning of the hearts. There can be no lasting change if the hearts of people are not affected and turned around. The indication is that the heart is in the wrong place and it needs to be turned. The Scripture declares, *"Out of the heart are the issues of life."* So if the issues of life are messed up, the heart is messed up. Only Almighty God has the power to reach deep into the heart. So this turn around, must be brought about by the move of God.

There must be a turning because things have gone in the wrong direction and the turning must be related to the heart. A resolution, often made at the turn of the New Year, endeavors to change action, but unless the heart is changed, there will be no change. The move of God goes deeper than any reason, strength of will or intellect can go. Resolutions will not bring a transformation. This move of God goes past the mind and the emotions and turns the innermost part of your being. If the heart is not touched and changed, then actions cannot be changed. So the move of God goes deeper than any reason, strength of will or intellect can go, creating transformation from deep within the heart.

THE HEART CHANGE

If there is not a heart change, there is not a life change. All that is left is an intellectual, mental acceptance of spiritual things which brings no permanent change. It is purely surface and superficial and has no substance. So many are living lives of great information and their desire is always to receive more teaching, more knowledge. They are ever learning and never coming to knowledge. There is no transformation of life and no formation of life. There is form but no force; profession but no possession. Their lives are zeroed in on pleasing others and speaking from a purely mental perspective. Information that does not lead to transformation brings consternation. There is a subtle temptation to live in a sub-standard spiritual life that has nothing to do with the depths of heart change. It involves no responsibility and very little accountability. This is not the kind of life that we see Elijah living. He was the prophet of deeds so we see the realm of demonstration in his life. One of his tasks will be the turning of the hearts and this turning creates a demonstration of the power of Almighty God, because out of this heart are the issues of life. The right heart produces right living and this is the move that is produced by the Spirit of Elijah. There must be a turning point and it must begin in the heart, in the inner man. Our Lord really is the King of Hearts.

Mark 9:12 states: *"12 And he answered and told them, Elias verily cometh first, and restoreth all things; and how it is written of the Son of man, that he must suffer many things, and be set at nought."*

Jesus said that Elijah would come and bring the restoration of all things. Here in this text the work of Elijah now has to do with restoration. I definitely believe that we are in the time of restoration when Almighty God is empowering His people to take back what the devil has stolen. Joel speaks about the locust, the caterpillar, the canker worm and the palmer worm. One eats the fruit of the tree, one eats the bark of the tree, one eats the leaves of the tree and one eats the root of the tree. When those agents of devastation finish their work, there is no tree.

Joel 2: 25,26 states: *"25And I will restore to you the years that the locust hath eaten, the cankerworm, and the caterpillar, and the palmerworm, my great army which I sent among you. 26And ye shall eat in plenty, and be satisfied, and praise the name of the LORD your God, that hath dealt wondrously with you: and my people shall never be ashamed."*

God will restore what these harvest killers, these agents of destruction have eaten, but that is not where He stops. He says that He will restore the years that the cankerworm has eaten. It is one thing for God to give back what the enemies have eaten up and this He does with multiplication. It is quite another miracle for Him to restore the years. Moments, days, weeks, months and years that have been eaten up are restored by the power of the Almighty. I believe that this mission of restoration is desperately needed in the church today.

So we have an end-time move that is being defined in the Scripture. He will turn, so there will be repositioning. It will be a turning of the heart as God goes deeper than reason and intellect, He goes deeper than action, He goes to the heart. When turning takes place here, in the hearts it filters to everywhere. Loving what you should hate, and hating what you should love is a matter of heart. Emotional dysfunction and reversal are a matter of the heart and do we, have a quantity of that in the church. When considered carefully, this move, this turning, this restoration brings an answer to the major problems that confront us today.

Chapter 3

The Spirit of Elijah

Luke 1:17 states: *"¹⁷And he shall go before him in the spirit and power of Elias, to turn the hearts of the fathers to the children, and the disobedient to the wisdom of the just; to make ready a people prepared for the Lord."*

This scripture presents an amazing revelation. It says when John the Baptist came, he came in the Spirit and the power of Elijah. It says that he will turn the hearts of the fathers to the children, the disobedient to the just and make a people ready for the coming of the Lord. Here is a divine connection between God's people, the coming of the Lord and the move that prepares them. Whatever this Spirit of Elijah is, whatever this moves represents, it is the move that makes ready a people for the coming of the Lord. So it is of great importance that we understand what the Spirit of Elijah is so that we can begin to experience and flow in the mighty move of God.

We know of Elijah's importance in the Old Testament and we will be dealing in detail with this. We know that on the Mount of Transfiguration, he was there. We know that he physically comes in the tribulation with an amazing prophetic assignment as one of two witnesses. The Jews of old and today have held and still hold Elijah in a special place of importance. At their 'seder,' they leave a window open or a chair ajar for Elijah. They hope that he will come to usher in the Messianic era. Some people think that he will help in rebuilding the temple.

So what is the Spirit of Elijah? I approach this with great sobriety and watchfulness for I believe with all my heart that this presents a glorious truth to the body of Christ. As I mentioned earlier, for many years, 10-12 years, this revelation has been in my heart and this is the first time I have released it in written form.

John the Baptist came in the spirit and power of Elijah so we know that the Spirit of Elijah is associated with power. When John the Baptist came we know that he was the forerunner of Christ. So it follows that this Spirit of Elijah will be the forerunner move that will precede the rapture of the church. Just as John the Baptist was the forerunner of the first coming, the Spirit of Elijah will be the forerunner of the rapture of the church. When John came he came with the message of turning, returning, repenting. So too this move of the Spirit of Elijah speaks of turning the hearts of men. John the Baptist stood against the religious crew that was against the Word of God. So too this Spirit of Elijah, this move has nothing to do with the man-made, liturgical, tenets of religion.

DEFINING THE END TIME MOVE

What is the Spirit of Elijah? The Spirit of Elijah is a move of God that comes in the power of the Holy Spirit that is related to the life, works and mission of Elijah. Elijah becomes the prototype, or example of ministry, spiritual life and mission before the rapture of the church. The spirit of Elijah represents the moving of the Holy Spirit, as He creates in us, aspects of the life of Elijah. There were experiences that Elijah had that will become personal experiences in our lives. There is a pattern and a process that he followed that will be a pattern and process that we follow. There were confrontations and victories that he had that God made prophetic so that they would become personal to us. So Elijah becomes a prophetic pattern becomes the guideline for ministry, spiritual development and end-time manifestation. To understand this, you must understand all you can about the life of Elijah.

Almighty God has chosen to repeat some of the aspects of Elijah's life in the future, tribulation period. The process he, Elijah, went through becomes a prophetic pattern that gives astonishing insight into present day, spiritual life. It puts into great perspective, the things that God's people are going through. It also gives predictive truth about things that will happen because this Elijah pattern becomes prophetic to our lives.

For the purpose of this book I will show you the absolutely powerful relevance of this pattern to our lives. It is God's will for you to understand what you are going through. God's will for your life is given to be known, not hidden, to be manifested, not overlooked. So the Spirit of Elijah is the Holy Spirit taking life lessons, mission manifestations of power from Elijah's life in the Old Testament and making them substance to you. Your life will then begin to reflect some of the aspects of Elijah's life.

Think about this sequence. Elijah came from relative obscurity he did not belong to the inner circle of the 12 tribes and he came from Gilead. Hosea 6:8 says, "...A city of them that work iniquity." Hosea calls Gilead a city of evil doers as being a rendezvous for wicked men, to express the thought that the whole land was full of evil doers. Elijah belonged to this wicked land where evil doers made their home. Yet out of this oppressive, hostile environment, the Almighty God would bring one of, if not the most powerful prophets in the Old Testament.

It would seem as though one of the reasons for his unrelenting, dynamic and potent life was that he came from such deprived, depraved circumstances. He transferred that warring, confrontational attitude to dealing with spiritual evils. He exhibited a no tolerance, no compromise, message that was reflected in his deeds. He is known, as we have said, as the prophet of deeds. We have so many prophets of words today and not too many that have these words translated into vital and potent action. No one could argue with Elijah when he was on Mt. Carmel and fire fell. No one could argue when he raise the widow's son. No one could argue when the widow's oil and meal were multiplied. No one could argue when the rain was shut off for three years. He approached life and ministry with seriousness and sobriety. He would not be intimidated by the rulers of the nation neither would he cower in fear when he was outnumbered on Mt. Carmel. He was not for sale and would not bow to the pressures of Ahab.

Here it is that an entire nation was plunged into abysmal darkness where altars were broken down. The flames from the lamps of witnesses were all but gone and it seemed as though a nation would be swallowed by idolatry. It was here, at this zero hour, that God raised a man with thunder in his voice to turn the tide of idolatry. When it seems that every attack of the enemy is about to swallow a nation and the people of God seem to be irrelevant, somewhere, God is about to raise a witness. When the devil has raised his vilest prodigies, Almighty God will reveal His Elijahs to stem the godless tide. Yes, he came out of obscurity and suddenly appeared.

It is high time for the people of God to stop placing the emphasis on the evil witness that is all around. The time has come to realize that the Almighty is revealing His Elijahs because He will not allow the flame of His witness to be extinguished. It is my firm belief that God is revealing these men and women that are filled with the Spirit of Elijah in this day. The evil tide seems to be at its highest level and the force of the enemy and his attacks on the people of God are at their peak. But now, today, in this moment, the move to bring these Elijahs to the front has begun.

NOT THE HUMAN MODEL

These men and women that God is raising, don't follow the carnal pattern of the superstar. They are not the ones who are highly approved by the upper echelon of ministry, neither are they the ones who are lauded by the upper crust of society. These are ordinary people who have come from a hidden place, not recognized by many, but have been saved for this moment.

The disciples that were chosen by Jesus, demonstrate this point with precision. Most of them were called from a fishing boat life, were living in obscurity, and were called out by the Lord to become city changers, nation takers and history shapers. God delights in choosing those who do not seem to have the credentials or carry the appearance. Do you thing that you have been living in obscurity? Do you feel that God has a supernatural call on your life? Do you feel that you have not fulfilled the potential that God has ordained for you? Let none of those things rob you of your expectation and belief that Almighty God is doing things behind the scenes that you do not know about.

Elijah was a Tishbite. He did not belong to the inner circle of the 12 tribes of Israel. He did not have any visible, glorious credential. He was not greatly approved by those in position. He was not known because of his association, so he was not a person of great reputation. This is something that has concerned so many in the realm of church life. There is an emphasis on association, whom you know and where you have been. Titles have become extremely important to many in so far that the use of the title is literally demanded. A title is not who you are; it represents what you do. Too many are enamored by the applause and the approval to the point that their lives operate in a realm of appearance.

In some areas of ministry today, I have witnessed this nauseating addiction to titles that carries with it the atmosphere of idolatry. Attention is drawn to the individual not the Lord, and the emphasis is their position, not the Lord's Kingdom. Elijah had none of these idolatrous, self-seeking, self-promotion attitudes in relation to the beginning of His ministry.

He was called by God, raised by God and positioned by God. He came from Gilead.

THE DIVINE CONNECTION: ELIJAH – JOHN THE BAPTIST

By virtue of the references in the Bible, there is a definite connection between Elijah and John the Baptist. Thy both emerged from nowhere and came upon the scene with a prophetic voice. Elijah came from Gilead and John came from the community of the Essenes. They both emerged from the wilderness and burst on the scene with a message of power, turning and returning that affected the nation. Elijah began to deal with Ahab and John got the attention of Herod.

It will be seen in future chapters that Elijah and the Spirit of Elijah puts you in the position of dealing with rulers and ruling principalities. Elijah was targeted by Ahab's wife, Jezebel. She leveled unparalleled hatred against Elijah and she tried to get Ahab to act on this hatred for Elijah. So too, John the Baptist was the target of exceptional hatred from Herodias, Herod's wife. She was so controlled by this hatred that she asked Herod, via her daughter, Salome, for the head of John the Baptist.

The common thread that runs through Herodias and Jezebel and Ahab and Herod is astonishing. Ahab and Herod were commanded by their wives to target Elijah and John the Baptist respectively. Not only did they want their husbands to target these prophets but their desire was to kill them. In Elijah's case, he was the head of the school of the prophets. In John's case he was also the head of a move that would usher in the first coming of Jesus. In essence these women were after headship.

The headship of Elijah lay in his relationship to the school of the prophets as he led the prophetic movement. John the Baptist would be the head of the movement of preaching repentance, standing against the attacks of the carnal worldly order of the day. He was the one that preached about the coming of the Messiah and was the forerunner of Jesus. If these women could eliminate these men, then all the leaders that were under them, all their followers in Jezebel's and Herodias' mind, would be scattered, the movement would be killed and their message would be removed.

The presence of these two prophets meant opposition to and assault on the kingdoms of these pagan kings and their wives. . It meant a threat to their attempt to control, and dominate the atmosphere of the kingdom. The only solution was to eradicate this presence and now to a more subtle and seductive point. The presence of headship, the presence of the prophets, meant that there were people that stood up against the king, their husbands. Because of their driven desire to have their husbands in total subjugation to them, anyone who threatened their position of control, would become a target for annihilation. Jezebel and Herodias embodied that hell inspired, Satan spawned hatred of the prophets.

THEY ARE AFTER
THE PROPHETIC MOVE

Jezebel embarked on a war against the prophets of God and Herodias singularly targeted John. In both cases, they were not only after the prophets but the prophetic move. Remember in the book of Revelation, the Bible says Jezebel claimed to be a prophetess. Wow! The scope of this godless spirit drove her to claim to have a position that was never given to her. This was her self-appointed, self-indulgent claim. The parallel is astonishing. May I submit this to you? If this spirit of Jezebel and Herodias is allowed to function without being exposed, the attack on God's prophetic move will be formidable.

This spirit is always connected predominantly to the idea of control but is only an element of the Spirit of Jezebel and Herodias. Understand that they needed the cooperation of their husbands in their campaigns. The campaign was to remove all headship including their husbands' headship. (Sir, do not abdicate your responsibility to have spiritual and physical headship in your home.) The move to kill the prophets and kill the prophetic move of God was the ultimate aim of Jezebel and Herodias. Elijah would bring Israel back to God and John would be the voice in the wilderness, and the forerunner of our Mighty Lord.

When I read and see that people have defined Jezebel and Herodias just by the word control, I must state that this is only partially true. These women were after the move of God, the movement of God and they were committed to kill whomever that move was coming through. Wherever the move of God is taking place, there is the place where this spirit will endeavor to lodge. Athaliah, the daughter of Jezebel, carried the same spirit and went after all the royal seed.

MOTHER AND DAUGHTER

Athaliah was the daughter of Ahab and Jezebel. She was determined to seat herself upon the throne of David. She attempted to kill all of the royal seed but Joash was hidden, and he escaped. What a diabolical similarity to her mother Jezebel. Jezebel was determined to be the power behind the king so that he would do her bidding. He would become a puppet to the whims of his wife. Athaliah was determined to do all she could to be seated upon the throne of David. Jezebel went after the prophets of God with murderous intent and with demonic venom. Athaliah, her daughter went after the royal seed to wipe them out thereby destroying any hope of future righteous rule. What a sinister similarity in the spirit and intent of mother and daughter.

When people indulge in this behavior, they fail to think about the impact it has on the people who are the closest to them. Athaliah was a killer and so was Jezebel. She desired authority that was not hers and so did Jezebel. She attacked anything that had to do with the God of Abraham, Isaac and Jacob and so did her daughter. Her actions, her attitude, her life were reproduced in the life of her daughter. The thought must be, are you comfortable with your attitude and actions being reproduced in those who are the closest to you? Your ability to influence lives, shape destinies and affect the future of those who are in your inner circle must be of vital importance to you. Jezebel transferred her spirit to her daughter and the family life continued in its evil and rebellious acts against the God of Heaven.

HEROD

There is another thought that absolutely confirms this. When Jesus was born, the move of God to touch the world through a Savior began. The wise men came from the East following the star and the star came and rested over the place where Jesus was and here the Magi bowed and worshipped the Lord.

The application is that all personal stardom stops where Jesus is.

However, on their way to worship the king, the Magi were stopped by Herod. Please understand that when you are on the right road, following the right star, heading in the right direction, you will be stopped. Herod told the wise men that when they found Jesus, they should bring Him the news because he claimed that he wanted to come and worship Him. Herod had absolutely no desire to worship

Jesus. His aim was to kill Jesus because he was afraid of the future threat to his throne. He wanted to kill what the Holy Spirit had birthed so that the mission of the first coming would be aborted. The devil is out to kill what the Holy Spirit is birthing so that the mission God has appointed will be eliminated. Herod, in the context, pretended to be a worshipper to get close to Jesus to kill Him. Beware of people who have the words, carry out the motions and pretend to be worshippers. Their only desire is to kill what God is doing and the Holy Spirit is birthing.

Now even though Jezebel and Herodias were consumed with desire to kill the prophets, they had to have the help of Ahab and Herod. These were the men with the signet rings of authority that had to be pawns in the hands of these anointing-killers. I know that many of you have seen unbridled hatred and inexplicable venom develop in church life between a very few and prophetic leadership. The anointing in prophetic leadership cast a curse upon Jezebel and Herodias and exposed them for what they were - prophetic killers. Because of this their attack on prophetic ministry was without parallel, without reservation and without control.

If Elijah were killed what would happen to the school of the prophets? If John the Baptist were killed what would happen to the forerunner move of turning and returning and repentance? In Elijah's case, the move of bringing a nation to God would be destroyed. In John's case, the move of repentance heralding the coming of Jesus would be annulled. These women were ultimately after the move of God.

SUBMISSION –
THE SPIRITUAL BATTLE

The prophetic move of God involves a spiritual battle, a spiritual battle of the deepest nature thus the Biblical teaching on the Spirit of Elijah, again becomes vitally important. The prophetic move of God demands submission to the Holy Spirit and in this submitting, authority from Heaven is seen. You can only exercise authority to the degree to which you submit to authority. So the inability to exercise authority in the believer, is the evidence of the lack of the ability to submit to authority.

When the spirit of Jezebel and Herodias are examined carefully, when their mission and purpose are exposed, the attack really is revealed as a spiritual attack.

With all the names, descriptions and definitions that have been given to this in years gone by, the essence and ultimate aim of their attack is the elimination of the spiritual move.

I find it fascinating that the move of Elijah and the spirit of Elijah has to do with the turning of the hearts which is a deeply spiritual move as we discussed in a previous chapter. You say the word submission in the church and immediately some people have a flesh-flag raised. This word has been equated with inequality, chauvinism, going back in time and many other expressions. It simply means that some people will not submit to any type of authority in the church.

The position of authority of the 5 fold ministry has been set by Almighty God, so it is not rebellion against a man when we oppose the 5 fold ministry but against the Sovereignty of God. It is astonishing to see people submitting to authority in the arenas of their job, the store, the police officer, but come into the church and refuse to submit to the authority structure set up by God in the church. This exposes the attempt of the enemy to abort the spiritual move of God that empowers people to be launched into the harvest.

The work of the devil is to do all that he can to create a lack of submission and introduce disorder so that this end-time move of God is stopped. God is a

God of order and His move follows that order. It is submission to God's order that opens the door to enter into the realm of God's operation. The level of submission will determine the level of the flow of God's power. God will never do His work in the realm of disobedience, rebellion and disorder.

All through the Scripture, from the order of the days of creation right through to the throne room in Revelation 4 and 5, order is seen. The attack on submission is a well calculated attempt of the devil to play on and manipulate the fleshly desire of man to be independent of God's law and so abort the move of God as disorder ensues. Do not buy into the fleshly and the carnal seduction. James 4:7 states it is in submission to God that you are enabled to resist the devil and he will flee. The devil will use any tool, manipulate any emotion, to cause you not to have the ability to resist him. The attack on your submission to the authority of God or to the God-appointed structure of leadership in the church is a subtle attack of the enemy. I say with all due respect that this is God's house. God has set leaders in His house and that structure is not left for negotiation or debate.

If you do not go to the CEO of the company you work for and negotiate or debate the structure of the company, why should this be so aggressively pursued in church life. It follows no reasonable logic because if this attitude is not shown in the work place, why should it be so frequently seen in the church. Yes sir, yes madam, it is the subtle veiled attack of the enemy who desperately wants to stop the spiritual move of the Almighty God.

There are times when people in church life develop the star complex. Because of their gifts, they become legends in their own minds and become consumed by their giftedness. Because of this, attention is drawn to them, their gift not the giver of the gift. Recognition, glory, honor must always go to God who is the giver of all good gifts. But when the glory is redirected to an individual, it reveals a base and vile attitude. The star rested over the place where Jesus was and I declare that all personal stardom must stop where Jesus is. No matter how bright the light, how great the star, its purpose is to point to Jesus.

Chapter 4

The Attack of Jezebel and Herodias

I believe with all my heart that this end time move of God is the Spirit of Elijah move. If as I suggest, the attack against it is not the attack of a person but the attack of a spirit, then only a move of the Holy Spirit can bring the victory over this. Here is the point that I must make, which I will do in the form of a few questions. Have you seen the spirit of Jezebel and Herodias in operation? Have you seen this operation increasing in frequency? Have you seen the inexplicable hatred of some for genuine, prophetic leadership? Have you observed that sometimes it comes from people pretending to be worshippers? Have some of these tried to get close to you to have you join in their godless campaign? Have you seen a lack of submission of some or many to God-appointed authority?

I submit to you that those who are a part of this are after the prophetic move of God so they target the one that God has appointed to birth and carry the move. They are anointing-killers and my advice to them is to beware because Jezebel died the way she lived. She was eaten by dogs.

Remember, the wise men never went back to Herod. You cannot avoid the first contact with these types but you can avoid further contact that can become a dangerous liaison.

Jezebel and Herodias will try to kill anything that causes their husbands to submit to anything but them. The life of submission is an offense to them thus this word 'submission' has taken on a world of negatives in church life. They have subtly infused their spirit into the fabric of church life and now this resistance to Godly submission has become very visible. This spirit has transcended church life and has invaded the home life and now marriages are assaulted by this same spirit. From the marriage, it has infected the lives of the children because the example before them has been so vivid and visible.

Many children have been taught this rebellion and have caught this lack of submission as they have seen and observed parental attitudes. If mother has refused to submit to spiritual or even marital authority and husband is just a mere figure head and does not take His position as the leader of his home, then a severe problem arises. I do not mean that all rebellion in children comes from this, but I do declare that when this attitude of lack of submission and rebellion is seen and heard by the children, it will become a part of their lives. I cannot ask my children to be what I am not. You teach some by what you say, more by what you do but all by who you are. Your character speaks so loudly that I can't hear your words. Please understand that the enemy wants to destroy your life, create dysfunction emotionally, devastate your relationships and destroy your home. This is a manifestation of the heinous, vicious, evil being that the devil is.

Let me put this in plain language. If you want your children to submit to parental authority, then you must be willing to submit to godly authority. To live a life of a lack of submission to godly authority and rebelliousness to God's structure, is to follow the base appetites of flesh and live in bondage to the satanic elements of independence from God and addiction to self. This is not the kind of life that I want to live or the kind of life I want reproduced in those that are around me. When Herodias said that she wanted John's head, it was a demand to destroy headship so that everything that headship produced, would be aborted. This demand came from the closest connection to the king - his wife, and it was the same with Jezebel.

WHO IS HERODIAS?
WHAT DOES SHE WANT?

Matthew 14:1-12 states: *"At that time Herod the tetrarch heard of the fame of Jesus, [2] And said unto his servants, This is John the Baptist; he is risen from the dead; and therefore mighty works do shew forth themselves in him. [3] For Herod had laid hold on John, and bound him, and put him in prison for Herodias' sake, his brother Philip's wife. [4] For John said unto him, It is not lawful for thee to have her. [5] And when he would have put him to death, he feared the multitude, because they counted him as a prophet. [6] But when Herod's birthday was kept, the daughter of Herodias danced before them, and pleased Herod. [7] Whereupon he promised with an oath to give her whatsoever she would ask. [8] And she, being before instructed of her mother, said, Give me here John the Baptist's head in a charger. [9] And the king was sorry: nevertheless for the oath's sake, and them which sat with him at meat, he commanded it to be given her. [10] And he sent, and beheaded John in the prison. [11] And his head was brought in a charger, and given to the damsel: and she brought it to her mother. [12] And his disciples came, and took up the body, and buried it, and went and told Jesus."*

Herodias was Herod's brother's wife. John told Herod uncompromisingly that he could not have his brother's wife. John took a spiritual stand before King Herod and would not be tempted to dilute his stand or change his mind. Herod would have put John to death but feared because the people counted John as a prophet. When there was a celebration for Herod's birthday, the daughter of Herodias danced before the king and it pleased him. He then promised to give to this daughter of Herodias, whatever she asked of him.

This entire scenario was well planned by Herodias. Before the daughter went to Herod, Herodias convinced her daughter to ask Herod for the head of John the Baptist. She knew that when her daughter danced, Herod would ask this particular question. Herodias was not in a position to dance before the King, so she got her daughter to do it. She was not in the position to ask for the beheading of John, so she got her daughter to do it. The man who took a stand for God, who was unafraid to declare the word of God, must be beheaded. If she could have the head of John, then maybe fear would take over and the move that John led, would be stopped. Instead the exact opposite took place. As our Lord was ushered in, miracles began to flow with the feeding of the 5,000, to Jesus walking on water, to the faith of the Canaanite woman, and the list of miracles goes on.

Just as Herodias was able to recruit someone to join in her unholy plot, so too that same controlling spirit recruits the gullible in the church world today. To recruit people to stand with this spirit, the devil employs all the operations of the flesh -negative, destructive criticism, murmuring, rebellion, personal exaltation, the attitude of superiority, the attitude of the 'S,S,S', the super spirit syndrome. These are but a few evils that Satan uses. These are some of the things that are used by the devil to recruit people in church life to stand in direct opposition to the move of Almighty God. The ultimate aim of this spirit is to destroy all that God is doing or plans to do. This spirit will use any means, cloak itself in any garb, adopt any semblance of religiosity take any position to recruit others to extend its filthy, destructive ambition. However, God always gives people who have been deceived and seduced by this spirit, a space to repent. If they only knew that by submitting their lives to this evil, they are treating with malice, the things of God. If they only knew that when they dare to touch the anointing with fleshly attitudes, or to touch the man or woman that God has anointed, they are leveling their attack against God Himself. These are probably not thoughts that cross their mind because deception and seduction point then in other directions. Let this be the moment when you are sobered, awakened and restored by the Spirit of Almighty God.

I WANT HEADSHIP

This satanically inspired, subtle move is the last attempt of the enemy to rob us of the harvest before the rapture of the church. If headship is assaulted, if leadership is scattered, then the vision to touch the world cannot be focused upon. If most of the efforts of the Pastor are focused on dealing with divisiveness among his leaders, then no vision can be implemented.

This spirit of Jezebel and Herodias is after the harvest, and will do anything, employ any deception, capitalize on any fleshly trait to do this. Why did Herodias make this heinous request to murder the prophet? All this man was doing was preparing the way for Jesus. The move that Jesus would bring would be integrally connected to the Kingdom of God and an army would emerge that would lead to the world being dramatically touched. The Satanic plan was to get rid of John and instill fear and panic in his followers: the thought was kill John, scatter the people and maybe, this movement of God through John would be destroyed. Here also lay a subtle cloaked attack. If John were killed as the forerunner of Jesus, the coming Messiah, then the way would be prepared to stop any movement of the Almighty God that He would endeavor to introduce through the Messiah. The ultimate aim of this vitriolic and violent spirit is always to destroy God's move.

We know how this entire plot turned out. John was beheaded, Jesus emerged, thousands followed Him, and the Roman Empire was touched by the power of God.

Jezebel's hatred and rage dramatically increased after Carmel. After the blood of her prophets ran down the Kishon brook, after the nation of Israel was brought back to God, and after the fire fell, her rage was fueled. She launched an all-out campaign to kill the prophet Elijah and endeavored to undo what the Almighty had just done mightily on Mt. Carmel. When she launched this campaign against Elijah and the prophets, Elijah ran.

A GOOD RUN IS
BETTER THAN A BAD STAND

Many of us criticize Elijah for running from Jezebel but there are times when a good run is better than a bad stand. When he ran feeling overwhelmed and overcome, dismayed and discouraged, he had an encounter with the angel of the Lord. Elijah, up to this point of running, had a dramatic impact on the nation of Israel. The kingdom of Ahab and Jezebel suffered under the anointed words and deeds of God's chosen servant. A spiritual siege was laid on the lives of these leaders and their priests, their false prophets suffered and many were killed. The demonstration of God's power on Mt. Carmel remains one of the most dramatic outpourings of God's power in the entire word of God. Many are very critical of Elijah for running from Jezebel after such a move of God. I will not try to explain or rationalize this act of running.

I must say this, even in this act of running, he was not running from God. Herein lies the sovereign mercy and the supreme majesty of our awesome God. On the run, Elijah had an encounter with God that would cause this prophetic move to be perpetuated through the 7,000 hidden ones. Maybe, someone who will read this book has had times of glorious impact. Maybe you have had a Carmel experience where spiritual enemies were destroyed. Yet for some reason you have found yourself running, fleeing, endeavoring to escape something or someone. Fear not my dear friend. Be assured that your days are not finished and your impact is not diminished. You will run into a dramatic encounter with God where life will be restored. I make no personal claims to any title, for they are not important to me. But as I write this book, I feel the prophetic, thus saith the Lord declaration. In some of the times when I felt, that the best impact of my life was behind me, a miracle happened. Restoration, reclamation, renewal came because of a dramatic encounter with our merciful, awesome God. Thank you my Father for loving us so that you give mercy when we deserve justice. Nothing else compares to this word called mercy. On that hill of Calvary, we see mercy. Wow! Thank you, Thank you!!

It was at this point of running, at the nadir of his life, that he was told that he was not alone, and that Jezebel would not be allowed to take away the prophetic witness. He was told that there were 7,000 left and the report on them was amazing. They were in hiding and they had never bowed their knees to Baal nor kissed the face of Baal. The angel of the Lord told Elijah that they were left for the Lord. They were not left for Elijah's program but for God. In being left for God, in being hidden, protected and reserved for God, they were now ready for God's mission.

Too many times we make our plans, initiate our programs, develop our methods then ask God to come and bless them. This was not the case here. Before all this attack of the enemy, the Almighty God had planned the protection of the 7,000, and kept them for the moment of their revelation. Note that in spite of Jezebel's attack, hatred and avowed purpose to kill the prophet and the prophetic movement, the angel of the Lord appeared to Elijah. This spirit of murder, this purpose of destruction will never, never stop the prophetic revelation of Almighty God. It was this unseen remnant that would perpetuate the move of God and Jezebel had no power to stop this.

The similarities of Jezebel and Herodias, Ahab and Herod are astonishing. In this hour, when the enemy thought that victory was in his grasp, once again, Almighty God staged a supernatural drama. Elijah was physically present in the Old Testament, and the spirit of Elijah came upon John the Baptist in the New Testament.

EXTERNAL PRESSURE AND INTERNAL DIVISION

I do believe that before the rapture of the Church there will be a genuine out pouring of the Holy Spirit as I have stated before. I also believe that the devil knows that this move of God cannot be stopped or affected by external pressure. When the devil launched a persecution through the 10 emperors of Rome, on the early church, much blood was shed. However, the blood of the martyrs became the seed of the church and in the midst of this campaign of evil, the church grew and multiplied.

When we study the book of Acts further though, we see the method of attack changed as the enemy tried to divide the church doctrinally and thus attack it internally. His plan then was to so divide the church internally, that the vision of touching the world would be canceled. This too did not work because of the doctrines taught by Paul, Peter, James,

John and many others and as seen in the Epistles, the Church continues to flourish.

Today, as we are living in the hope of the imminent return of Jesus, it seems as though this attack is being replayed. So much confusion has been introduced into the internal aspects of church life, and church leadership. There are several doctrinal differences that have developed over the last several years. There are many that may question the need for the power of the Holy Spirit to be manifested in the church. Others feel like the church must adapt its message to the times so it becomes more accepted and more palatable. Many say that there is no need to emphasize the blood because it is not necessary to portray a bloody, slaughter house gospel. Many say the church must become more seeker friendly (or user friendly) so the face of the church must be changed.

I declare, without hesitation, that the message of the church must always be that the blood of Jesus cleanses from all sin. That the Holy Spirit is free to do what He wants when He wants, where He wants. This is God's house and not a man's house. This is God's work, not a man's work. This is God's kingdom not a man's kingdom. You assume a position that is not yours to take when you choose to dictate the way

God moves. It is actually a dangerous position that will turn the church into a club when your will and way, replace His will and His way. Saying that, I believe that God's move will be a move of order not chaos and confusion. If I am accused of preaching a bloody gospel, I plead guilty. If it is said of me that I believe in the power of the Holy Spirit, I certainly do.

Many pastors are so absorbed with dealing with these attacks that they have no drive, or desire to fulfill the commission to which they are called. However, in this zero hour, Almighty God is raising a remnant and it is obvious to me that this is happening around the world.

There is an indifference in many churches to touching the world. Instead, there is an absorption with physical things.

Matthew 28: 18-20 states: *"18 And Jesus came and spake unto them, saying, All power is given unto me in heaven and in earth. 19 Go ye therefore, and teach all nations, baptizing them in the name of the Father, and of the Son, and of the Holy Ghost: 20 Teaching them to observe all things whatsoever I have commanded you: and, lo, I am with you always, even unto the end of the world. Amen."*

This is a clear command of our Lord as He gave His disciples final instructions before His ascension. Being His final words, they were potent words that must be followed. Go ye into all the world, teach all nations. Jesus' final wish was to focus His disciples on touching and impacting the world. Today many do not go to the world, they tell the world to come to the church. So many are trapped by the cares of the life that they are immobilized by the worldly grasp on their lives. The absorption with self-will, self-promotion, self-welfare has become so overpowering, that the commission of Christ has become the omission of His people.

GOD'S COMMISSION – MAN'S OMISSION

Just before Jesus departed this earth, He left instructions for the church. What was the great commission of Jesus, has become the great omission of the people. He said to go: the Christians pray that they come. He said make disciples: we say make a comfortable version of Christianity. What has been affected so fatally is the very reason for being born again: Why does fanatical Islam display such fervor and zeal to fulfill their commission to kill, and the Christian show so little fervor and zeal? Why do other religions display such engagement that they walk the streets and Christians, generally speaking, are at ease in Zion?

It seems as though most of the Christian world schedules the work of the kingdom around the hobbies or habits of their life. While other religions are out doing the work of their cause, many Christians are enjoying the fishing expeditions and indulging in the pastimes of life. I am not saying that these things are wrong because I believe that there must be recreation in life. The problem comes where there is little or no engagement in the affairs of the kingdom and an almost total absorption with self interests.

When the priority of kingdom work is replaced with the priority of self-interest, a great violation to the word of God has been committed. We must develop socially because God requires balance in our lives. However, this social development must not be at the expense of spiritual development. The priorities of life must be placed in the right place. I have said before that the priorities decide the pursuits. You will aggressively pursue what the priorities dictate. When there is visible evidence that people pursue the social aspects of life or the acquisition of material things, then you can be assured that their priorities are in this direction. I say again, that the recreational aspects of life are of extreme importance but they too must conform to Biblical standards. I myself like to play the game of golf and I certainly enjoy taking Renee, my wife to the movies when we can. When I am at home my wife knows where I will be at 3:00 p.m. in our home. I will have the television on, watching Bonanza. I happen to like western movies. I myself, enjoy these recreations of life but they do not take precedence over the spiritual priorities of life.

We boast of greater power than these false religions but they do the spreading of their gospel. We say that we love Him, but not enough to touch a world. We say that our desire is to see others go to Heaven but not enough to evangelize our communities. We, with a casual approach, and a cavalier attitude have placed the responsibility to touch the world squarely on the shoulders of 5 fold ministry. What has caused such apathy and indifference? How have so many become content with good that they never strive for the best? I submit to you that an internal attack has been leveled with subtlety and seduction against the hearts and minds of God's people. The Scripture states that out of the heart come the issues of life, so life issues emanate from the condition of the heart.

It now becomes prophetically significant and personally transforming when we read that the spirit of Elijah turns the heart. Note that the internal attack goes beyond what is seen, straight to the innermost being of the Christian, the heart, mental warfare, emotional attack and a spiritual assault have become consistent in the life of today's believer. I am convinced that the answer to all of this was prophesied when God declared that the last move before the coming of the Messiah would include the turning of hearts.

So many desire to see the external manifestation of God's power and so do I. But I long to see an internal revival, where things that have died internally, spring to life. I long to see internal restoration where things that the enemy has stolen: wholeness, joy, peace and power are restored. Yes, the spirit of Jezebel and Herodias have launched an attack internally, which lets you know that the devil is aware that a mighty move is being born. In fact I believe that this attack is already here. But I also believe that this attack does not speak of the devil's power as much as of the devil's panic. He does not know the future but he does understand prophetic patterns. So he knows that there is reason to panic.

IDOLATRY IN THE CHURCH

It is not only that abomination and idolatry and demonic activity have filled our world but here is the presence of this idolatry within church life. Whatever commands your highest devotion that becomes your god. As we have said, the priorities of so many in the church are centered around themselves, their puny worlds and their personal dreams. The things of the Kingdom have been relegated to a secondary position. To many, the Holy Spirit is like Jonah in the belly of the ship-only called up in the time of crisis. I repeat, so many church people have become apathetic and indifferent to the great commission. They have adjusted the Word to accommodate their lifestyles instead of adjusting their lifestyles to be in accordance with the Word. By their purposes, priorities and passions they have framed their own Christ. They feel falsely safe in the crucible of their own idolatry and can justify their lack of commitment and passion for the Almighty God. Prayer services are almost empty, Sunday night services are canceled and meetings in church have been crunched in. Imposed time-constraint time constraints are the norm. There are few appeals for the lost to be saved and post service altar times are all but gone.

The nation of Israel in the Old Testament was given the law, the covenants, the promises, the ark. They were given the only continuing manifestation of the glory of God, the pillar of cloud, the pillar of fire and they were given the priesthood. How could they degenerate into such darkness, abomination and idolatry? How could they become so immersed in the worship of Baal and Ashteroth with the blaspheming priests all around them? How could they lose their fervency for God, lose their purpose and be reduced to idolaters? How can so many, that had so much become so alienated?

ATTACK IN PEW AND PULPIT

Think of the parallel to church life today. We have the Word of God, the New Covenant, the anointing of the Holy Spirit, the Blood of Jesus, the Name of Jesus and the death, burial and resurrection of Jesus. The list of our blessings is endless yet so many have become so weakened, so deterred and detoured, so sadly seduced. How could such a deterioration take place in the midst of so much promise?

As if this were not enough, here is another parallel to this idolatry today. Men of God, preachers of the Word have been overwhelmed by materialism, overrun by possession and have put a price tag on their gift of grace. A gift, freely given by a sovereign Lord, now begs a dollar value. Many are more concerned with things than with the Kingdom of God. God wants us to have things, but things must not have us. When ministry is governed by the acquisition of things, by the hunger for possession, and the desire to solidify one's own position, we now become hirelings. I understand the concept of budget, expenses and life, but when this supersedes all else, something is drastically wrong. When attitudes, world gimmicks, world programs and world spirit are visible in ministry, it ceases to be ministry.

In the Old Testament, the Ark of God could not be brought in on a Philistinian Cart. A worldly method cannot usher in God's presence. Father, help us all, as Your servants, to understand that all we are is because of Your mercy to us. Whatever gifts, whatever calling, they are not ours but have been given to us by You. We are but stewards, not owners. Please do not sell your future for your present, your inheritance for a pot of beans like Esau.

The parallels between the conditions in the time of Elijah and the conditions today are almost exact. Yet in that time, from nowhere, suddenly, Elijah emerged with a word from Heaven that would impact a nation. I know that there are men and women like this that have been in the background, in the hiding place sequestered until this time. I am praying that a word from God will trigger a dynamic sequence of prophetic events in your life so that suddenly, there will be an emergence of God's hidden, chosen.

PARALLELS BETWEEN THE FIRST COMING AND THE SECOND COMING

When Jesus came the first time, He came to be a born of a woman. When He comes the second time, He will come as King of Kings and Lord of Lords. When He came the first time he came as Savior, when He comes the second time, He will come as undisputed Master. When He comes the second time the world will be impacted. The first time, His words were words of mercy, grace, and glory. When He comes the second time, His word will be as a sword and a flame of fire. When He came the first time it was to shed His blood. When He comes the second time it will be to unclench the fist of Gentile rebellion. When He came the first time, it led Him to Calvary, when He comes the second time it will lead Him to the Millennium. When He came the first time, Herod tried to kill Him, when He comes the second time, no power will lay a hold of Him.

When the church is taken out at the rapture, she will not be a weak, spiritless, anemic, fearful, cowering church. I submit to you that no power or force, internal and external shall stop Almighty God from raising a remnant who will be used to bring a move of enormous power to the world. So here is the important point. Will you be one of those who will press past the superficial, press past the self absorption of the renegade flesh, press past the temptation to rebel against Godly submission? Will you be one of those who will not be controlled or dominated by the spirit of Jezebel or the spirit of Herodias? Will you be one of those who will not stage an upheaval against headship? My prayer is that you will be one of those that the Almighty will use in a mighty way. The spiritual move of the Spirit of Elijah is already here and oh, how on time, how desperately needed, how absolutely relevant is this move to our lives. Be filled, be flooded and flow in the glory of this move of God.

Chapter 5

Elijah's Life —
A Prophetic Pattern

Having dealt with a definition of the Spirit of Elijah and the necessity of this move we now begin a marvelous journey. This journey will take us through a series of prophetic revelations that are given about Elijah's life. These revelations are prophetic in that they become substance and a reality to us today.

His life becomes a God-chosen prototype or model to understand some of the things that will take place in our lives. If there is one person in the Bible that fully represents a pattern that will give us our life lesson, it is Elijah. His life brings great insight into the process of our lives today. It becomes a visible definition of what we have been through, what we are going through and what is about to happen. I have always said that the will of God is not to be mysterious and unrevealed. Its purpose is to give us revelation to live by, thus, we do not live in darkness and ignorance.

Elijah is mentioned in key, prophetically significant events in the New Testament. On the Mount of Transfiguration, he was there. He will return in the Tribulation lest God, *"smite the Earth with a curse."* I believe that he will be one of the two witnesses. Some Jews believe that he will assist in the rebuilding of temple. Now, long before this happens in the Tribulation period, we have the Spirit of Elijah coming upon John the Baptist. This was so evident that many thought he was Elijah. The thought is this. What Elijah will be in the Tribulation with all the demonstration and purpose, will be created before the rapture, by the Spirit of Elijah. It will be just as the Spirit of Elijah infused John and empowered him to be the forerunner of Jesus, our Messiah.

It is not that some ghost of Elijah will appear. It is that the Holy Spirit, by His power, person and purpose will create in the lives of God's people, patterns, experiences and demonstrations that characterized Elijah's life. Literally, you will see a repetition of the breakouts and breakthroughs that filled Elijah's life. This is evidenced by the way John the Baptist was earlier infused by the Spirit of Elijah and used and also by the miracles that will be revealed in the Tribulation period through Elijah. Why is it so easy to believe that this Elijah life pattern can be repeated in the Tribulation period but it will not be seen before the rapture? I say, that God will never be left without a witness and a remnant. I declare that the spirit of Jezebel or Herodias will never become the final say. I say that the Ahabs and Herods will never be able to stop the mighty prophetic move of the Almighty. To understand the nature of this Pre-Rapture move, the purpose of this move and the definition of this move we must journey through the life of Elijah. We must begin from his emergence to his translation.

I was interviewed on television concerning this revelation and had over 48,000 hits on my website in one night. Many of the comments were similar in nature. The thing they had in common was gratitude for the definition of the Spirit of Elijah. Many sing about it, talk about it, but now is the time to understand it and define it. Let us begin this revelation journey.

WHAT'S IN THE NAME?

I Kings 17:1 states: *"And Elijah the Tish-bite, who was of the inhabitants of Gilead, said unto Ahab, As the LORD God of Israel liveth, before whom I stand, there shall not be dew nor rain these years, but according to my word."*

This begins a revelation on Elijah that is absolutely filled with dramatic interventions. It begins with the name "Elijah, The Tishbite." To understand the full scope of what the Spirit of Elijah represents, we must carefully understand the revelation contained in his name. God chose to identify the name of Elijah to represent and define the end-time move of the Almighty. As great a leader as Moses was, as daring a soldier as Joshua was, as remarkable a king as David was, it was Elijah who was chosen to exemplify the end-time move of God.

Names in the Bible were always given to show the intent of God, and to clearly define what this particular life would accomplish. The name Adam means Earthly, or taken out of Red Earth and so Adam became the head of the Earthly race. Eve meant living, so she became the mother of the living. Abraham means the father of a great multitude so he became the father of the Jewish nation. Joshua means the Lord, the Savior so he became the one whom the Lord used to bring Israel into the land and the list goes on and on. Many times in the Word of God, a name revealed the intent of God. The name Elijah and its meaning now becomes particularly powerful and enormously significant in relation to the future. This name means, "The Lord is strong, or the Lord is my strength."

Before we comment on this name, it is of extreme importance that we understand the context in which Elijah emerged. He literally burst on to the scene with absolutely no reference to genealogy. No reference is made to his father or mother so that we know that he did not come with great pedigree. Credentials and pedigree seem to have become very important in today's church, and Elijah had neither. He may have been excluded by the hierarchy of today that has become so infatuated with titles. I have actually been exposed to situations in ministry where certain ministers insist on being called by certain titles. So insistent were they, that they became incensed if those titles were not used. How pathetic that some only derive significance from a title. Maybe this partially explains why in some realms of ministry, there is such a lack of the demonstration of the power of God.

Elijah, though, burst on the scene and began to speak with power and authority. This happened almost overnight. Consider the context of his emergence. The valleys were filled with erected altars where false prophets howled to Baal and Ashteroth. Idolatry filled the landscape of this nation and a carpet of gloom and darkness benighted the land. Think of these altars to the true God which had now been profaned. As the smoke billowed from evil sacrifices, think of the stench in the nostrils of God. Think of the darkness when there should have been light, think of the darkness when there should have been holiness. A nation swallowed and consumed by its own idolatry and vicious sin. Here, in the midst of this affront to the Almighty, in the midst of this great darkness, here, a man suddenly emerges with no great description of who he is. He is simply called Elijah, The Tishbite.

THE LORD IS MY STRENGTH

What's in a name? Elijah - God is strong, the Lord is my strength. Here begins the wonderful journey of a man, with no great pedigree, with no human credentials, destined to be used to change a nation. Isn't this an absolute parallel of what is happening today? False prophets of New Ageism, humanism, materialism, universalism have filled our world. They scream across the media and they yell on our campuses. Darkness has engulfed this world as men have sought to eliminate the name of God from school systems. They have tried to take the Ten Commandments out of our courtrooms. They have even sought to take the name of God out of The Declaration of Independence. Deep idolatry fills this land and our world as mankind has endeavored to create its own puny gods. The resemblance to today, is astonishing. Yet in this moment, the Almighty is moving in a special way. The Lord is strong, the Lord will be your strength.

As Elijah burst on to the scene, he had to be a man of exceptional strength and courage. He appeared in the midst of overwhelming odds and in an atmosphere that was seething with rebellion and chaos. Here, the Lord was saying, I am your strength, I will stand before you and with you. Baal, Ashteroth and the other puny gods will not stand in my way as I show who I am through My chosen vessel. There was a supernatural union between Elijah and the Almighty God so that who God is would be seen through the life of Elijah.

It was not just that God was giving to Elijah but that Almighty God was standing with him. This was a serious hour, with unparalleled evil, with a hateful king and a venomous wife. This was not the hour for servants of partial commitment for servants that were faint of heart. It was the time for confrontation of confusion, the time of the heavenly intervention when hell seemed to have vomited out its vilest minions. With a king who was one of the most wicked if not the most wicked in Israel's history, with a wife, Jezebel, who swore to wipe out the prophets of Israel, this was no time for surface saints. And here comes Elijah, suddenly, quickly, with a heaven sent, supernatural, God-empowered word contained in the name, THE LORD IS MY STRENGTH.

I have always said that this end-time move would be a quick one. I have said that the day of the superstar, title addicted, personal kingdom-builder person is over. Elijah came suddenly and he came with no human approval, applause or acknowledgement. Once again, I call your attention to the phrase, *"THE SPIRIT OF ELIJAH."*

SPIRIT vs. SPIRIT

The idolatry of this time was deeply rooted in spiritism and demonism so that the worship of false gods literally opened the mouth of hell. Only the Holy Spirit working and moving could contravene and intervene in this spiritual chaos. Thus this move of the Spirit of Elijah would be more than able to combat, to overcome, to overwhelm these idolatrous altars. Let me reiterate, God chose a man from a nowhere place, from a no described family, with no pedigree, to lead His move. Isn't this just like our Almighty God? People will choose the powerful, the wise, the visibly endowed, but our God chooses someone that no one else would choose.

There are so many prophetic lessons that become personal at this moment. Do you feel that God has greatness for you? Do you know that you are destined to be used mightily? Do you feel unqualified? Do you feel that you have no pedigree or human credential? Do you feel that you did not come from the right place? Amazingly, the things that you feel disqualify you, are the things that actually qualify you. God magnifies Himself from littleness to greatness, from death to life, from nothingness to something, from darkness to light. Here comes Elijah as an astonishing example of the end-time move of God. God will be your strength, He will make you strong, He will be your defense and offense.

It seems as though today's society is a replica of the idolatrous rule of Ahab and Jezebel. It seems as though much of church life demonstrates materialism where the acquiring of things has become more important than the commission to go and make disciples and touch the world. It seems as though many have tried to humanize God and deify man (make man a god). Here in this evil called humanism there is no need for an absolute standard. Thus there is no need for total obedience and accountability. People in this realm frame their own realities and draught their own narratives. Ahabs and Jezebels are rising up all around to countermand the word of the Almighty and to target for death those whom the Almighty has chosen. So now, it is not only where is the God of Elijah but where are the Elijahs of God?

AN EXPERIENCE
IN A PASTOR'S OFFICE

It is quite unusual for me to share a personal experience but I feel compelled to share this one, so please indulge me.

It is not very often that I have been in a Pastor's office and have received a direct, precise, prophetic word from God. In fact I will say this is the first time this has happened in over 39 years of ministry as of this writing. It was my first visit to this church in North Carolina and I was ushered into the Pastor's office to visit. Little did I know what was about to happen. For about 12 years this revelation on Elijah had been a major part of my life. Really it is more like 15 years. I breathed this, studied this but somehow was not released to write about it. It was not because the desire was not there.

The Pastor walked into his office and we began to speak. It took me all of 5 minutes to know that this was an extremely unusual servant of God with sharp, prophetic understanding. As the conversation continued, he began to speak about Elijah and about the spirit of Elijah. I was immediately focused on what he was saying to the point where I lifted my both hands and stopped him. I took out one of my cards that was made for a meeting that I have in Tulsa, OK every 4-6 weeks as of this writing. The card said, 'The Elijah 7000'. The synergy that developed in that office in minutes was astonishing. As you can imagine, we became instantly bonded by the Holy Spirit and revelation that had been given to both of us.

It seems as though The Almighty joined us together that morning in a very unique way. He then made a statement that prophetically confirmed so many things in me. He said to me that there are very few people that he knows that carry The Spirit of Elijah. Then he said, 'It is not only where is the God of Elijah, but where are The Elijahs of God?' Then he looked me in the eyes and said, 'This morning you are God's Elijah to this body. Welcome!' I cannot tell you the flood of emotion that absolutely flowed through me in that office. Where are The Elijahs of God? This pastor had never met me, just knew a little about me, and yet gave me one of the sharpest, most relevant prophetic words that I have ever been given. It seems as though that was the "sudden" moment that something in me was triggered. After years of study, years of speaking on The Spirit of Elijah, this trigger point was so powerful that I was now loosed to write. I will always have a special prophetic connection to this special servant of God and I say to you, "Pastor, Thank you."

Chapter 6

Divine Intervention to Sudden Appearance

Now remember I have written about the spiritual condition in the time of Elijah. See the heathen altars, the billowing smoke from these altars, the blasphemy, the satanic priesthood, the canopy of enormous darkness. See the rebellious people, the unspeakable abominations and the almost total corruption of the land. Then suddenly, here stands Elijah with a word from God that brings the power of Heaven into the corrupt abomination of this idolatrous land.

Ahab was a ruler that possessed military ability and was able to defend his territory. He took to the battlefield and won and built up cities and the economy of the country. However, he did not value the ideas of moral and spiritual well-being. So what did he do? He adapted the modern moves of the day and brought the pagan customs of the region to prominence. He became a spiritually deluded, spiritually bankrupt king that was a negligent and indolent ruler.

When Elijah came into direct confrontation with Ahab, he, Elijah was filled with indignation and jealousy for the name of his God. In his mind the covenant that God made with Israel was the epicenter of its well-being. Without this, wealth and military might were a hollow things. Any king who would disregard the covenant of God, build images to false monstrous gods, and pursue material things would lead the nation into delusion. Elijah repudiated, he rejected, and he renounced this gutless king that was a puppet of an idolatrous wife. He defended Israel's covenant with the Almighty God, with his life as his words contained no compromise. He would not be intimidated by pomp or pageantry, by robe or regalia. Ahab represented the civil and religious authority of the day but this desert dweller, this mountain inhabitant, this prophet with no letters of recommendation would stand before Ahab. And here, in this stand, Ahab would find out who Jehovah God was.

MORE PARALLELS

Let us consider some parallels.

Ahab had considerable ability and talent but saw no value in establishing morality and spiritual well-being. There are some in church who have talents, gifts and abilities but are not interested in a spiritual move. They have become very satisfied with accomplishments and abilities and have no desire to go into a deeper relationship with God. Being content with the superficial things, the importance of spiritual things has disappeared. Occupation with the material world has become the priority of their lives and the acquisition of things has eliminated their desire and hunger for spiritual things. Ahab brought a dimension of material wealth to the nation but was not interested in anything that had to do with the Almighty God. Beware of the peril of placing priority on things because it is the beginning of a dangerous sequence of events that lead to a downward spiral.

WORLDLY MOVES

Ahab then adapted the modern moves of the day. There, another mistake was made. The spiritual elite endeavored to bring in the presence of the Almighty

God by employing natural and worldly methods. There are so many that borrow the methods of the world to translate them into church life. It is believed that if they do this, it will attract a different group of people. But in doing this, another realm of seduction is opened that will bring great deception. When Ahab adopted these worldly maneuvers, it led to the introduction of pagan customs, the building of pagan altars and the erection of pagan houses to worship their evil gods.

Here lay the ultimate goal of Satan. It is found in his age old desire to be worshipped. The introduction of these pagan altars and pagan gods was a result of the loss of value of moral and spiritual well-being, followed by the introduction of modern worldly moves and methods. The procession of evil that followed, took a nation to the brink of disaster. Oh how the pagan altars of materialism and humanism have been subtly erected in church life! These practices are very common to life in the world but have no part of life in the house of the Almighty God. In simple language, the worship of these modern-day pagan gods means that even in the halls of church life, some emphasize material things more than the things of God.

THE RIGHTS OF MAN
VS.
THE RIGHTS OF GOD

It is regrettable that some emphasize their rights more than the rights of God. Some live according to their will more than submitting to the will of God. Some adjust the Word of God to fit their lifestyle and do not adjust their lifestyle to the word of God. Life becomes a life of spiritual convenience. It becomes a cross less, costless life, where there is no need to crucify the flesh, there is no cost, and no responsibility. Spiritual things have no priority or so little priority, that the affairs of their lives are more important than all else. Here in the holy corridors of God's house, in some lives, God has no priority. Remember, it is the priority that determines the pursuit. Now we understand why so many aggressively pursue the things of the world more than the things of God. This may seem as a simple, accepted thing, but at the root is the attempt of the enemy to get Christians bowing at the pagan altars.

The material things, the cares of life, the worldly stuff gives a very hollow texture to life. True life is found only in the covenant of God, in truly following God and in commitment to Almighty God. When these things that characterize the world take the place of spiritual things, then the enemy has succeeded in creating pagan altars and pagan worship. So we return to Elijah, whose emergence from total obscurity was sudden and powerful. His first act after his introduction was His stand before King Ahab declaring that there would be no rain on Ahab's kingdom for these years. He not only declared that the heavens would be shut but he declared the time period that it would be shut. This was a sudden intervention from God through a man that was not known. I recall the moment when I was in that pastor's office. It was as though that spirit was in that office. I felt in a matter of moments something supernatural was triggered. As I mentioned, I personally felt a release of revelation in my life that led me to the writing of this book.

Some of you have been praying, worshipping and working in the midst of assault, oppression and darkness. You may have felt that your greatest days are behind you. You may have felt that you have no pedigree, no credentials and no titles. I declare prophetically to you that His work of bringing you to the place that He wants you to be, will be sudden. Elijah's word after his sudden appearance, brought a direct intervention from Heaven. God reserves the right and exercises His Divine prerogative to work suddenly. Again, you have always heard that this end-time work will be a quick one and I really believe this to be true. It will not come the way you thing it should or through whom you think it should. No one, no one legislates to God as to whom, how, where and when. He is the Almighty and His ways are higher than ours. I am certain that this Pastor and I will have future encounters that will be related to this Spirit of Elijah move.

THE TISHBITE FROM GILEAD

The word Tishbite means 'He that makes captives'. It was the name given to Elijah derived from the name of the town Thisbe in Gilead beyond Jordan. This area in the mountains was reputed for its palms but was also overrun with idolatrous altars and saturated with abominations and evil. Spiritism and demonism filled the land and it was close to the land of the Gergesenes where Jesus cast out the devils which He sent into the swine. So here is the question. Why would someone take up his residence in a place like this? This was also the country of the Amorites which compounded the evil for they were one of the major enemies of Israel.

We can only imagine that Elijah lived under uncommonly, difficult conditions with a low standard of living in this rocky, mountainous region. In the midst of what the world would perceive as the disadvantaged, the poor, the unfortunate, Almighty God was preparing a man for His mission.

How glorious is the sovereignty of God that He can locate a man in the mountain of Gilead, prepare this man who is surrounded by evil, and then bring that man to a place of prophetic destiny. Elijah did not live in the ideal place nor did he have the ideal education, but he was prepared by God. How gloriously ironic that a man that was not exposed to deeper or higher education would be the head of the school of the prophets. How prophetically significant that this man, surrounded by false altars, would rebuild altars in Israel.

What a prophetic lesson taught to us all at the beginning of the record of this man's life.

Chapter 7

Elijah the Tishbite

Elijah was a Tishbite, living in the mountains, surrounded by idolatry, right in the midst of the Amorites. The Bible speaks about the iniquities of the Amorites who were mainly engaged in spiritism. The word Amorites means 'bitter'. This is the place that Elijah came from. So an ideal location has little to do with the move of God. Let it be known that whatever you have been through, wherever you have come from, whatever you were surrounded by, Almighty God will locate you. When man's system, man's knowledge and man's perspective frown on you, the Almighty has only just begun to do His mighty work in you. One of the greatest Old Testament prophets, in my opinion the greatest, was located by God, prepared by God, commissioned by God to have supernatural impact on an entire nation. The sovereignty of God is infinitely superior to the intelligence of man.

I remind you that the word Tishbite when translated means, 'He who makes captives.' I am stating that the Spirit of Elijah must be understood in the context of Elijah's life. Life blessings, demonstrations, processes that Elijah went through, must become a prophetic pattern for your life. Here understanding can be attained by observing the life patterns of Elijah.

So Godly intent begins with the name, Elijah the Tishbite, 'He who makes captive.' This really is reflected in the life of Elijah. He faced the prophets of Jezebel, the prophets of the grove, priests that were seduced into idolatry. He faced demonic powers that had overrun a nation, and a king and his wife that vehemently hated God's people. Yet in the midst of this, fire fell. He was able, with the help of God to make captive all the forces of the enemy that were running unchecked and renegade over Israel.

The following pages will show you that his life was filled with demonstrable lessons that were an illustration of his name. Enemies of the Almighty God would fall before Him. Overwhelming odds and abominations would be against Him but He would not flinch. He would not be moved by the forces that were external because he had a revelation of God that was deeply internal. That internal revelation was infinitely more powerful than all the external forces that came against him. The attack of the enemy was without question, the result of the stand that he took for God. Never allow the forces that seem to be numerically superior on the outside, daunt you. Greater is he that is in you than He that is in the world.

Elijah's life was lived with the knowledge, that every force that tried to capture him would itself be captured. No enemy was too great, no force too formidable, no odds too prohibitive, no king too powerful. His position was: I know where I came from, and in those days of preparation in the mountains of Gilead, the hostile forces that surrounded me could not destroy me. Now I stand with the direct commission of God, so I will declare who He is and we will see what He will do. All of this in a name? Elijah," the Lord who is strong," or "Jehovah is my strength."

What a declaration of the omnipotent God being vitally engaged in the affairs of his life. He did not just prepare me or commission me, He is with me. He does not just enable me, HE IS WITH ME. With

Elijah there was a sense, a recognition, a deep knowledge that the Almighty God was with Him. If God be for me, who can be against me. He carried that more than a conqueror, God is able, I will not be destroyed mindset into the processes of His life. I will not be captive. I would like to say, I will make captives. I would like to say, I will make captives, the things that have tried to make me captive. Idolatry, abomination, false gods, blasphemous priests and corrupt altars all live on the attack. The aim of these evils was to make Israel a captive but Elijah's life was summed up in these words. *"The Lord is my strength,"* and He will cause me to make captives. The things that were on the attack to make me captive will now be made captive because the Lord is my strength. The puny false gods of Baal and Ashteroth, the godless priests, the false prophets will be made desolate. Their plans will not come to fruition. The people of the Lord who were captured, will be released by the power of Almighty God. All illustrated in a name.

ELIJAH'S DAY AND TODAY

When you read the chapters preceding 1 Kings 17, there is no mention of Elijah. You read instead, of the building of the temple of Solomon and his presumption in taking foreign wives. You read of the flood of evil and idolatry that filled the land after his death. You read of the fighting between Jeroboam and Rehoboam. The land was divided between the North and the South and only the Tribe of Judah and the Tribe of Benjamin remained true and formed the Kingdom of Judah while the other 10 tribes revolted and formed the Kingdom of Israel. The idolaters in Israel surpassed the imaginable and in the midst of these torrents of idolatry, these floods of abomination, Ahab and his wife Jezebel rose to the throne. The condition was perilous, the idolatry was open and blatant and Israel was in peril. The covenanted became the conquered and the chosen were carried away into the literal house of Satan. And now, in the space of one verse, 1Kings 17:1, here comes Elijah.

I submit to you that there are many prophetic parallels to your life today. I submit that there is a repetition of prophetic principles that is obvious.

We are facing today the same type of idolatry, except today it screams from every aspect of life. It is carried by the media, taught in universities, studied in colleges, upheld in major institutions. It seems that anywhere you turn, blatant idolatry, the rejection of Almighty God and opposition to Jesus Christ by the spirit of the antichrist is visible and aggressive. So many feel so daunted by the enormity of the challenge, that they have been robbed of the desire to do anything. There has been little response from most Christians to this evil presence. The Christian world analyzes it, debates about it and has gathered all the statistics about it. But in reality, it has done very little in relation to responding to it and counteracting it. Evil has been allowed to have free reign because of the apathy and indifference of many. It is as though the intelligent assessment, the flowery evaluations have rocked the church to sleep in the lap of this current abomination.

Now here it is, here is the hope and the response, THE SPIRIT OF ELIJAH! Elijah faced all of this in his day and after idolatry displayed its fullest evil, Almighty God began a miraculous work.

NO LONGER HELD CAPTIVE
BUT MAKING CAPTIVES

Yes, the Lord is your strength my friend, and He will empower you to make captives. These forces, these world framed doctrines, these demonic forces and this full potency of evil that have tried to capture you, now you capture it. There is a remnant that is not a numerical majority that still has this heart. I am convinced that in the moment when the devil raises his vilest prodigies, somewhere, God has reserved men and women to be raised in the crisis hour. Welcome Elijah! I will never forget those words. They still pierce my heart while writing this chapter on a Monday morning at 4:45 am.

The pastor that told me this called yesterday. We had a wonderful conversation and my respect for him grows. There are wonderful people of God that are just waiting for that moment of revelation.

The crisis of today demands no delay, the move must not be postponed nor must you go into the administrative chambers and plan the move with long term, short term or medium term objectives. The evil is present, the danger is clear, the idolatry is progressive, and the false gods are landed. Now Sir, now Madam, ARISE! Some have been told that you are a loser, that you can never win, that you will ever excel and that you will never rise to the position that God has ordained for you. Why have you believed the lie? I do not look through the lens of what is around me, I look through the lens of what God has called me to, through His Word, His power. You carry the hope within you and what the world needs now, what the church needs now, more desperately than even before, is for the Elijahs to arise.

Spirit of Elijah, flow freely through those who have no pedigree, no credentials, no introductions. So dear brother, dear sister, the waiting period is over. Let your lamps be lit with the divine witness. Let the fires of revival and restoration rise with their highest flames. Let the remnant be silent and hidden no more. Let the church arise so that never again as a covenanted, chosen people, will we allow hell to rise? Never again will our silence allow idolatry to be increased. Never again will we be bludgeoned into submission to defeated enemies. Spirit of Elijah, flow freely for I am here, available, ready, willing to take the stand.

Elijah came with no formal introduction, no fore-runner and no army behind him. He just emerged. Yes, the Spirit of Elijah, the Tishbite, of the inhabitants of Gilead, is here.

Chapter 8

Deepest Idolatry and Loudest Voice

So Elijah comes from nowhere, presenting no authorization papers from earthly authority, and immediately begins to speak. He does not diplomatically give his preamble neither does he hesitate to begin declaring with authority. It would be interesting to know what would cause a man to be filled with fearlessness to declare a word from heaven. Remember the situation that prevailed in the land. Solomon had had his indulgence with his foreign wives, his sons at his death fought each other bitterly. The 12 tribes were split into 2 regions, the southern kingdom Judah, and the Northern kingdom, Israel. Israel had degenerated into unimaginable idolatry and the false prophets of Ahab and Jezebel had run roughshod over the entire nation.

It seems impossible to believe that a king of Israel, Jeroboam created a type of idolatry that is so mind defying. He was afraid that the people would keep some affiliation and connection to the temple, and this worship of the true God would erode his power. Yes, the connection to the temple, the true worship of the true God would erode idolatry. This is why the tribes of Judah and Benjamin in the kingdom of Judah would not bow to the false gods. Jeroboam was afraid that if any semblance of connection existed to the true God, eventually his people would return to the house of David. To ensure that this people were swallowed and controlled by idolatry, to ensure the bondage and the continuation of the false worship, this king of Israel committed an unthinkable act.

THE DEEPEST IDOLATRY

1 Kings 12:25-33 states: *"25 Then Jeroboam built Shechem in mount Ephraim, and dwelt therein; and went out from thence, and built Penuel. 26 And Jeroboam said in his heart, Now shall the kingdom return to the*

house of David: ²⁷ *If this people go up to do sacrifice in the house of the* LORD *at Jerusalem, then shall the heart of this people turn again unto their lord, even unto Rehoboam king of Judah, and they shall kill me, and go again to Rehoboam king of Judah.* ²⁸ *Whereupon the king took counsel, and made two calves of gold, and said unto them, It is too much for you to go up to Jerusalem: behold thy gods, O Israel, which brought thee up out of the land of Egypt.* ²⁹ *And he set the one in Bethel, and the other put he in Dan.* ³⁰ *And this thing became a sin: for the people went to worship before the one, even unto Dan.* ³¹ *And he made a house of high places, and made priests of the lowest of the people, which were not of the sons of Levi.* ³² *And Jeroboam ordained a feast in the eighth month, on the fifteenth day of the month, like unto the feast that is in Judah, and he offered upon the altar. So did he in Bethel, sacrificing unto the calves that he had made: and he placed in Bethel the priests of the high places which he had made.* ³³ *So he offered upon the altar which he had made in Bethel the fifteenth day of the eighth month, even in the month which he had devised of his own heart; and ordained a feast unto the children of Israel: and he offered upon the altar, and burnt incense."*

He said if the people go to sacrifice in Jerusalem their hearts would be turned to the Lord. See here the context of the Spirit of Elijah and the turning of the hearts. Jeroboam knew as long as there was a longing in their hearts to go to Jerusalem, he would lose his hold on them. Let it be known today, in the midst of the mayhem and the condition of many in the church, there is still a longing for worship in some. As long as this is there, idolatry will never be able to have its full impact. The king was determined to wipe this out of the heart of the people. Again the attack was on the hearts of the people. Protect the heart sir, protect the heart.

Jeroboam then made two calves of gold and he set one in Bethel and the other in Dan. Now the people with a weakened heart, with vile, vicious, idolatrous leadership, and now open idols, surrendered to this evil. He made priests of the lowest of people who were not of the sons of Levi. See the decline, see the deterioration, see the degeneration as a nation plummets to the abysmal depths of despicable idolatry. The lowest of people were chosen to be the priests and the altars to worship evil were put in the highest place. Your highest place is your heart and spirit and it is in this place that was created to worship God, that the enemy wants his altar, his idolatry, his abomination.

How can a king of Israel, someone who has seen the glory of the Lord become such a vile instrument in the hands of Satan? Yes, even back then, Satan would do anything, employ any method, introduce any idolatrous altar to get worship. Remember this! Every substitute, every erected altar, every temptation to bow to other puny gods is the attempt of the devil to get your worship. It is not just a giddy excursion in fleshliness, it is not just depraved humanity in its extreme. No, it is the direct attempt of the devil to replace God with himself.

Isaiah 14:12-14 states: "*₁₂How art thou fallen from heaven, O Lucifer, son of the morning! How art thou cut down to the ground, which didst weaken the nations! ₁₃For thou hast said in thine heart, I will ascend into heaven, I will exalt my throne above the stars of God: I will sit also upon the mount of the congregation, in the sides of the north: ₁₄I will ascend above the heights of the clouds; I will be like the most High."*

Yes, here the desire of Lucifer is unmasked. He said in his heart, yes, I will ascend, I will exalt, I will sit, I will ascend, I will be like the Most High God. These five 'I wills' were all centered around the dethronement of Lucifer. He no longer wanted to be the worshipper, he wanted to be the worshipped. Please hear these words today. Whenever you are tempted to live the 'I will', independent from God, self-important, self-absorbed life, it will culminate in the realm of trying to be your own little god. Your will, your renegade passion will endeavor to remove the notion of absolute authority so you have no need to submit. See the common thread in satanic operation when the 'I will' becomes the only law to which you submit. This should be a herald to church life, that all the 'I will' attitudes that are so clearly seen, even in leadership, inevitably end in the erection of fake altars. But the deepest idolatry occurs when you bow to the altar of self.

REDIRECTED WORSHIP

Jeroboam endeavored to replace the cherubim with golden calves so that worship that was meant for God would be redirected to the devil. So many have got caught up in the trivial things of life, have devoted their time, their talent, their resources to purposeless pursuits. This is the subtle idolatry, as dangerous as any other type, that has infiltrated a realm of church life. Can you believe it? Little gods created with the hands of people to create a lifestyle that is acceptable and accommodating to fleshly desire. Yes, this happens, even in the house of God. May God help us all. Jeroboam said that if the people went to sacrifice in Jerusalem, it could affect their hearts. Oh yes, this worship is a heart thing, it is the insulation to idolatry. True worshippers never bow to the puny, handmade gods of man.

Then Jeroboam said that if they sacrificed in Jerusalem they would turn to their Lord. Notice the words that should now be familiar to you: hearts and turning. Then Jeroboam said that if they turned to the Lord, they would kill him. So to protect this life of abomination, he introduced idolatry among God's people. He was right, if they turned to God, if they followed their heart to Jerusalem, idolatry would be killed.

The attack to make Christians worshipless, is the attempt to preserve the life of idolatry. It is so difficult to understand why it becomes hard for people to have a spontaneous praise in the house of God. Worship leaders have to instruct people, request of people to lift up their hands and open their mouths to give praise to the Almighty. Even when this is done, many refuse to engage in open praise to God. They never refuse to engage in open recreation, or open small talk, or open humor. Why should we have to prompt praise, or request the lifted hand?

REPLACE THE FEAST – STEAL THEIR WORSHIP

I declare that true worship is the acknowledgment of the worthiness of God and an open declaration that we will bow to no one, nothing but Almighty God. You must be thinking, "What does this have to do with the Spirit of Elijah?" Let us see. Jeroboam then ordained a feast in the eighth month, on the 15ᵗʰ day like unto the feast of Judah. He created his own feast like to the feast in Judah which was at the time, the Feast of Tabernacles. This feast time was the time of the dwelling in booths and this was a joyous time and points to the time in the future when God dwells with people in the millennial reign of 1,000 years. But here, the king created a feast for the dwelling of idolatry. It is the fullest extent of sin that someone would endeavor to replace the cherubim, build altars, appoint priests from the lowest order, then replace the feast. How the devil hates God, hates God's people, hates true worship. How the devil hates the dwelling of God in and with His people. I am including this record of Israel's history because this is the scene on to which Elijah emerged.

There were other kings after Jeroboam, Abijah became king of Judah walking in the sins of the father. Baasha became king of Israel and did evil in the sight of the Lord. Omri became king of Israel and he did evil in the sight of God and did worse than all that went before him. Then came Ahab, the son of Omri and Ahab did more to provoke the anger of the Lord than all the Kings that had gone before him. He reared up altars and built groves for idol-worship. Now you see the land, the history, the atmosphere and the scene upon which Elijah emerged. How could a man take such a position of power in a land that was overrun with false priests and idolatrous altars?

ELIJAH SPEAKS TO AHAB

Elijah now speaks, but he speaks to no one but Ahab. He goes straight to the throne. The word from the Lord that he delivers, is given to Ahab. Ahab is told that it is because of his evil and his wife's evil, it is because of their false gods that this has befallen this nation. Elijah's word was given straight to the king, not to some secondary powers. Here is Elijah, coming from the mountains of Gilead and his first act was directed to the most powerful man, speaking in human terms, in the entire world. There is no interaction, no shyness, no fumbling. It is a clear, direct, powerful word from Heaven from a prophet who has been prepared for this moment. I am sure that Elijah, while in the mountains of Gilead, where he was surrounded by evil, must have said, "When, when, will I be sent out of this place?" You never despise the time of preparation regardless of the length of time. You never leave the place of preparation no matter how adverse the surroundings.

So finally, in God's time, Elijah is revealed and he is revealed to the king. It is time for those who have been prepared, who have this anointing, the Spirit of Elijah, it is time to begin speaking to rulers. I do not just mean physical kings, but ruling principalities that have squatted on territories. They must be notified that the greater power is here. These ruling spirits must be notified that the word from God brings the highest authority. These principalities must be notified that divine intervention is here. To come from the mountains of Gilead to Ahab's throne speaks of a miraculous journey. Do not let the humanity of your beginning, the threatening circumstances around you or the presence of enemies alter your belief that God can take you to a high place. Elijah's beginnings were prophetic. In the town where he grew up, enemies surrounded him and these enemies were reputed for their indulgence in spiritism. They were a violent group and this city was a meeting place for all kinds of people of this sort. Even though this environment was terrible and the people were not interested in the God of Abraham, Isaac and Jacob, God had a supernatural plan in Elijah. So now comes his sudden emergence, his ascent to speak to King Ahab.

THE ELIJAH PATTERN – OUR LIFE

I believe the reason that Almighty God chose to pattern the end-time move after Elijah is that there is such an identification between our experience and his life. We find our purpose, our pattern to be reflected in this Spirit of Elijah move. It really is a movement that we are a part of taking us to our prophetic destiny. Think of those who feel that their season is gone because of the length of time that they have been in the mountains of Gilead. Think of the many for whom God has a supernatural tomorrow that feel swallowed by their surroundings. Think of those who feel disqualified because of their humble beginnings and their modest environment. Do we find specific identification with the record of Elijah's past, who he was and where he grew up? Out of all of the characters of the Old Testament none of them has the versatility, the extremes, the prophetic, ministry purposes as Elijah.

As we progress in this writing you will be amazed to see the depth and detail of Elijah's life reproduced in you. His struggles reflect your struggles, his processes reflect your processes, his confrontations reflect your confrontations and his ultimate victory reflects your ultimate victory.

THERE SHALL BE NO RAIN

It is not only that this man chosen by God and empowered by God spoke to Ahab. The first words of his public ministry are over-poweringly ominous. There shall be no rain on your kingdom, Ahab. Let me interpret. Ahab you have tried to stop the worship of Israel, you and your heinous wife have erected altars to your false Gods. You have made groves to honor your puny gods. You have introduced idolatry and abomination and done more to anger the Lord than any other king. Your evil is unparalleled and you have allowed your wife to have free reign to express her venom to the nation and against the true prophets of God. This is what you have done. Ahab, this is what my God will do. There will be no rain on your kingdom. The heavens are going to be shut and your kingdom will suffer. Ahab you have attacked and oppressed from an earthly level because you are an earthly King. You have imposed limits, though, on what you are able to do even though you think that you have free course to do whatever you want.

But my God who has chosen me and called me, is the Almighty God of Heaven and Earth. He is sovereign, supreme and supersedes all other authority and power. He has authorized me to shut the heavens. Your attack on God's people has been earthly but this judgment coming upon you is heavenly. See, Ahab, my authority, my word does not come from human government it comes from another world. It comes from Heaven and this is the authority that has the power to shut the heavens.

WHERE ARE
THE ELIJAHS OF GOD?

So here is this ex-inhabitant of the mountains beyond Jordan. Here is this ex-occupant of meager surroundings. Here is the man with no great human degree, credentials or introduction. He comes with no accompanying title. And here he is, shutting up the heaven over Ahab's kingdom. Ahab, with all his pomp and power, his regalia and splendor, has not a clue about opening and shutting the heavens. He does not have the power to do this but Elijah, the nobody, from the nowhere place, with no great title, shuts the heaven. Being interpreted, this means that there will be no blessing, no continuation, no prosperity on his kingdom. Ahab's, reign of terror, deception and oppression is about to come to an end. The chosen man, the anointed man, the called man was empowered so that the heavens could obey his word.

So, it is not only where is the God of Elijah, it is where are the Elijahs of God? Who is ready to rise to the place that God has destined for you? Who is ready to declare on an Ahab – Jezebel ruled world, that the heavens will be shut up because the prosperity of evil is about to be terminated? Homosexuality, lesbianism, pornography, teenage pregnancy, dope addiction, divorce, alcoholism and all other evils, judgment has come. Where are the Elijahs of God who have been called and chosen and now will speak. We will no longer be silent because of the throne of Ahab and Jezebel. The numerical odds that outnumber us on the earth are of no consequence. God's mathematics are different because 1 can put 1,000, 2 shall put 10,000 to flight. Heaven needs only a minority, only a few, to put many to flight. So many have been intimidated by the presence of the Ahabs and Jezebels. They have been silenced into submission because of fear. But something supernatural is happening in the body of Christ.

Chapter 9

Dangerous Alliances

The verse that introduces Ahab is;

1 Kings 16:30-33 which states: *"30 And Ahab the son of Omri did evil in the sight of the LORD above all that were before him. 31 And it came to pass, as if it had been a light thing for him to walk in the sins of Jeroboam the son of Nebat, that he took to wife Jezebel the daughter of Ethbaal king of the Zidonians, and went and served Baal, and worshipped him. 32 And he reared up an altar for Baal in the house of Baal, which he had built in Samaria. 33 And Ahab made a grove; and Ahab did more to provoke the LORD God of Israel to an-*

ger than all the kings of Israel that were before him."

The depth of Ahab's evil, his introduction of idols, his marriage, his cruel, idolatrous wife and his feebleness of character all add up to this introduction. Verses 31-33 continue the decadence of his life. It says with Syria being a menace and a threat, he decided to make a treaty with his neighboring nation, Phoencia. To seal this he married Jezebel, the daughter of Ethbaal, the king of Phoenicia. He willfully entered into this marriage because of the fear of Syria, and because he thought that this marriage would strengthen him. He did it in total disregard and in complete rebellion against the Word of God. Verse 31 says that he walked in, *"the sin of Jeroboam."* and this was not a light thing. However, in addition to this evil, he then married this queen of idolatry and turned to the gods of Baal and Asherah. The Scripture declares that this king Ahab went and served Baal, and worshipped him and reared up an altar of Baal. He built a house of Baal in his capital of Samaria, and there in the capital of Israel, abominable idolatry took place.

Not only did he consider the sin of Jeroboam trivial, he proved this by going to the next level of evil by marrying Jezebel. Not only did he build an altar for Baal in the temple of Israel but it is believed that he built Asherah's pole to honor the goddess of fertility. The Scripture says that Ahab did evil in the sight of God above all the kings before him. This seems to be a peculiar statement because the scripture said, that OMRI, who was the father of Ahab took the nation to a level of idolatry that was cruel, abominable and deep.

I am spending some time dealing with Ahab and the condition of the nation because this is the time which God chose to cause Elijah to emerge. This was the time that called for a sudden intervention with a level of demonstration that was astonishing.

PARALLELS BETWEEN AHAB'S TIME AND OUR TIME

Please consider the following parallels between Ahab's time and today when God said that He would send Elijah. Before the great and dreadful day of the Lord, we see a demonstration of miracles in the tribulation period. These miracles bear an exact resemblance to the miracles that were wrought by God through Elijah in 1 Kings. Now that we are dealing with the Spirit of Elijah, we must consider the spiritual, political and social conditions of our time. It is amazing to discover that the conditions that existed then are exactly replicated today. It all follows a prophetic pattern. Yes, the Spirit of Elijah versus the Spirit of Ahab and Jezebel, and the Spirit that has been infused by these godless, idolatrous, abominable leaders into the fabric of society. May God help us as Christians, as leaders, as people who are touched by the Holy Spirit to do all that we can to stop this spirit from infiltrating our lives.

Let us analyze these similarities:

1. As if walking in the sin of Jeroboam were not evil enough, Ahab married Jezebel for political expediency. The parallel is obvious. Today, much sin and failure of the past have been disregarded and an accommodation of worldliness, a treaty with materialism, an embrace of selfishness have begun to become characteristic of what we see in the realm of church life today. All this is done for the satisfaction and gratification of the baser element of sin and flesh. Ahab did this to protect his kingdom and so too today the kingdom of self and flesh is protected and perpetuated by

these fleshly liaisons. It seems as though vision has been eroded, standards and commitment have been diluted and the requirement of holy living has been totally replaced. Instead of adjusting life to conform to the Word, many have adjusted the Word to conform to their lives.

2. The second parallel is also obvious and highly visible. Ahab began to serve Baal, worshipped him, reared up an altar, and built a house, a temple of Baal in the capital of Israel, Samaria.

SERVANT – MASTER RELATIONSHIP

Let me give you a New Testament scripture about servants and masters;

Romans 6:16-23 states: *"16 Know ye not, that to whom ye yield yourselves servants to obey, his servants ye are to whom ye obey; whether of sin unto death, or of obedience unto righteousness? 17 But God be thanked, that ye were the servants of sin, but ye have obeyed from the heart that form of doctrine which was delivered you. [18] Being then made free from sin, ye became the servants of righteousness. [19] I speak after the manner of men because of the infirmity of your flesh: for as ye have yielded your members servants to uncleanness and to iniquity unto iniquity; even so now yield your members servants to righteousness unto holiness. [20] For when ye were the servants of sin, ye were free from righteousness. [21] What fruit had ye then in those things whereof ye are now ashamed? for the end of those things is death. [22] But now being made free from sin, and become servants to God, ye have your fruit unto holiness, and the end everlasting life. [23] For the wages of sin is death; but the gift of God is eternal life through Jesus Christ our Lord."*

People develop servant-master relationships and the Scripture is clear that to whom you yield yourselves, they become the masters. Some very serious questions have to be asked of Christians today. Who or what have you submitted yourself to and what has become your master? You have a servant-master relationship with something and someone. 1 Kings 16:31-33 gives a sequence of events. Ahab served Baal and worshipped him. Everyone worships someone or something because no one is a vacuum. You become a worshipper in direct correlation to whom you are serving or to what you have submitted. You must answer the question, what or who are people in the church worshipping? I am speaking generally because there are always remnant saints, be they few in number, that always represent the true worshipper.

In Revelation 11:1,2, the angel is commanded to measure the temple. Let me present a parallel to you. How does it make you feel to know that God is measuring your worship? When He does, what kind of measurement does He come up with? Does your worship come out of a voluntary submission to the most High God. Some of these questions are extremely difficult to answer and these challenges are very hard to confront. However if we allow this apathetic attitude to continue, this new wave of modern infection to go unchecked, then we will have a devastation of lives. We must not allow the enemy to rob us in our own house.

Is there a need for a restoring, reviving, reclaiming move of God? Men go fishing for hours, golf for hours, indulge in hobbies for hours, why should we place a specific time limit on the move of God. Why should we structure our services with such rigidity that if the midday time is passed, we have people leaving to get to the restaurants before the crowds, or we have people looking at the clock to remind the preacher that his time is up. Hours for ourselves and restricted time for God, His word, His move. Maybe this does not describe in anyway where you are at. If it doesn't, be thankful to Almighty God. We can carry on sustained energetic conversations for several minutes and in some cases several hours, but can only be in praise and worship for a few seconds. Please, consider this: To have to be prodded and prompted and pushed to lift the hand and open the mouth in praise is not the sign of a true worshipper.

THE ALTAR

Ahab then erected an altar to his god in the house he built for Baal. The altar was the place where the others would come and concentrate their worship and freely give their worship. It was the place where they felt they were closest to their god and sacrifices were made there. These altars are a prominent place in the exercise of the false religions. But originally, the altar was a place of sacrifice and worship to the true God. Altars were built all through the Old Testament - from the time the Ark rested on Mt. Ararat and Noah emerged, an altar was built. And so all through the Old Testament, the building of altars held a vital place. Elijah repaired a broken down altar and then fire fell. Ahab built a home for Baal but erected an altar so that others would be attracted to the false deity.

Where are the altars today? I know that prayer is not necessarily a physical posture but it is a condition of the heart. However there are certain attitudes that are taught in the Bible in relation to prayer, praise and worship. The bowing, the kneeling, the lifted hand, the open mouth are all indicative of prayer, praise and worship. I will say that in many churches today, there are no altars. After the message or sermon or sermonette is given, many places no longer give an appeal for salvation. Many do not have a time after the message where people can spend some time in devotion, prayer and rededication. The schedule is rushed, the service outline is held to with rigidity and the time of departure is pretty much set. I understand when a church has multiple services on a Sunday morning that a schedule must be followed but I also believe that no schedule should legislate to the Holy Spirit. Should God choose to do something in His house that is unusual, we should be sensible and sensitive enough to let Him have His way.

A HOUSE FOR BAAL –
IN THE CAPITAL OF ISRAEL

The Bible then continues this sequence with Ahab and says that he built this home for Baal in Samaria, the capital of Israel. In the land that was given the charge to be a light to the world, in the city that was made their capital, a house for Baal was constructed. In the place that was given to honor the true and living God the king built a house for the false deity, Baal. Again the parallel for today seems obvious. In the house of the Lord that is created to be dedicated for worship, that is created to be the center of God's operation to touch the world, something else has emerged.

In many churches, the mission is no longer touching the world. The standard is no longer holy living and the house that has been created to honor Almighty God, now stands to honor others. In God's own house in many places, people and things are more honored than Almighty God. Some leaders have become so reputation-driven, so titlepossessed, that they have declared that this is their territory and the people are their people. No, this is God's house, it is His territory and the people are God's people.

HONORING GOD

I believe in respecting and honoring the Pastor of the local church, but not at the expense of and to the exclusion of honoring Almighty God. To build a temple to another god in the place that is the capital of the country that God has chosen, is abominable. When you enter the house of God, let it be known that this is God's house. We are here to honor Him and all because of His worthiness. May people not build places within church life that will honor someone else at the exclusion of honoring God. He is first, He is greatly to be praised. Should leaders use the pulpit to solicit support for their egocentric delusional flesh trips? May we firmly stand against this idolatry in the house of God. Should leaders choose the path of building something for their recognition, their honor and put Almighty God in the last place in His house? May we vigorously with spiritual force oppose this. Should some desire the approval of man more than the approval of God? God help them to see that this is His house, where HE IS LORD.

AHAB DID EVIL:
ELIJAH SPOKE TO AHAB

All of these parallels that we have drawn between Ahab's time and our time, scream for the move of the Spirit of Elijah. We understand to a great degree why the emergence of Elijah was so sudden and so rapid and came, with such powerful demonstration. Serious conditions call for serious methods and God sovereignly chose to intervene with directness and force at this time in 1 Kings. Now, that you have seen some of the similarities between Elijah's time and ours, you can see the need for this move of the Spirit of Elijah today. When Ahab emerged, the scripture said, *"...he did evil in the sight of God above all that went before Him."*

When Elijah emerged with suddenness, he spoke directly to Ahab and brought with his word, a direct intervention of heaven. The time for limited responses, the time for weak reaction is over. The challenges are enormous, visible and they are aggressive. This is the time for the emergence of the people of God with boldness and fearlessness. I believe with all my heart that there have been people that were hidden in adverse circumstances that have been prepared for just this moment. Let the warriors arise! Let the remnant rise! Let the hidden be hidden no more. Almighty God is far above, infinitely higher and sovereignly more powerful that any ruler on his earth. It is this supreme God who has called and commissioned us, who will enable, equip and empower us. Before this glorious God, Ahab and Jezebel are but puppets. And Elijah spoke to Ahab!!!

BATTLE WITH
BAAL AND ASHERAH

1 Kings 17:1 states: *"And Elijah the Tishbite, who was of the inhabitants of Gilead, said unto Ahab, As the LORD God of Israel liveth, before whom I stand, there shall not be dew nor rain these years, but according to my word."*

Verse one introduces a huge segment of powerful revelation in relation to defining the Spirit of Elijah. We have already dealt with the beginning of the verse as we spoke of Elijah, the Tishbite of the inhabitants of Gilead. We also dealt with the implications of Elijah speaking to Ahab and now the discussion continues. This emergence of Elijah was so sudden, his stand so dramatic and his words to Ahab so filled with power that we must understand how he was able to do this. Elijah's approach did not follow the rules of diplomacy. In today's language, it is not the worldly acceptable norm to defy an established authority like this.

Let me explain a little further. These metal images of Baal were erected on the mountain of Israel. Here, the priests of Baal would commit the abominable act of child sacrifice. They would take the first born sons from the women of Israel then throw them into the flames. As mothers moaned and grieved and cried, these evil priests would cut themselves with knives and cry out to their false gods. As if this evil was not enough, they would have their ritualistic prostitutes and perversity, homosexual acts in honor of the goddess Asherah. Here the Asherah fertility poles were set up and the men of Israel would be involved in consorting with prostitutes. All of these acts were committed to honor the gods of Baal and Asherah and it brought torrents of evil and abominations to such a degree that it surpassed all idolatry before this time. It is in this terrible flood of falsehoods, idolatry and perversity that Elijah emerged.

Think about this for a moment. False gods erected in the high places, the killing of infants, perversity in morals, prostitution, all of this done to the honor of false gods. All of this sanctioned by the idolatrous beliefs of the day. And here is Elijah. What gave him the power to stand against this nationally sanctioned evil? What gave him the heart to go against an entire nation? What helped him to conquer fear and intimidation?

AS THE LORD LIVETH – BEFORE WHOM I STAND

"As the Lord liveth." These words are few but they are of immense significance with regard to the stand that Elijah would take. The gods of Baal and Asherah were dead but the God that Elijah represented was alive. He was able to mock the priests, and defame the false gods because he knew that His God was alive. It was the life of that God, infused into Elijah that was able to give him supernatural strength. The day in which Elijah lived, the demonstration that had to be made, the fearlessness with which he had to stand could only come from the living, supernatural God. In one moment of divine exchange, our living God, the God who liveth would give Elijah a touch that all of the false prophets put together could not come near having. Their yells, their screaming was of no consequence because their god was dead. They may have represented a

numerical majority but one man with the living God on his side became the majority.

The one thing that makes Christianity most distinctive, is the fact of resurrection. Our Jesus is alive forever more and has the keys to death and hell. It is this life that pulsated through the apostles to touch the Roman Empire. It was this life that caused them to spread the gospel to the then known world in spite of the persecution of the emperors. This is the life of the Almighty God given to His people that enables us to do supernatural things in the spirit world. He is the Lord God of Israel and He liveth.

A DYNAMIC AFFIRMATION

He is the God of Israel, so too, Elijah, He would say He is my God. This surpasses confession: it is now affirmation. He is not just Moses' God, or Joshua's God, or Abraham's God, He is my God. He is directly connected to me and I am directly connected to Him. All that He is can flow into all that I am because He is my God. Israel may have forgotten for a period of time about their God, but their God never forgot about the nation of Israel. This is what Elijah spoke to Ahab. He said, *"As the Lord God of Israel liveth."* You may be king here on earth, but the Almighty God, He is God of Israel. Your puny gods have no power to change the fact that Jehovah is our God. Elijah knew that he was personally and vitally connected to Almighty God. He knew that no earthly king, no erected idol, no backslidden nation could rob him of that divine connection. He came, he spoke because of his connection, commission and call of his God. This is something that Ahab, and the false priests could never understand.

1 Kings 17:2-24, 1 Kings 18:30-46 present a prophetic sequence in Elijah's life that is a major part of the prophetic pattern for your life. Here in these verses you will find specific identification of things that you have gone through and will go through. These verses become a textbook for direction, a dictionary for definition, and a source of prophetic utterance. It is my sincere desire to deal with this in detail so that his life lessons can be applied to your life. However, as the Spirit of Elijah revelation has been fleshed out, I find that 1 Kings 17:1 continues to be of paramount importance. This is the verse that records Elijah's introduction and the stand that he took.

HOW DOES HE STAND?

I will continue to carefully examine this verse because it gives us the reason why he was able to demonstrate this unique and magnificent, spiritual gallantry. Let us continue to deal with the sentence, "As the Lord God of Israel liveth." What does it really mean to know innately that the Lord God of Israel lives? It means that personal relationships, personal connection, personal communication are all possible. On Mt. Carmel his mocking of the false gods was based on the fact that their God could not hear that personal voice. His derision of Baal caused them to scream and shout even more and Elijah's response was that he must be on a journey or he must be asleep. There was no answer from Baal because he was a dead god forged from metal with the hands of men.

Think for a moment of what Elijah was doing before a watching nation of false priests, idols, false gods. The king was observing, the authorities were there and this lonely, single prophet is mocking the national god, instituted by man. Elijah knew that His God lived, that he had a personal relationship with Him. Elijah knew that he could talk to His God and this true God would answer him. As we progress through the life of Elijah, as we see the pattern of the Spirit of Elijah, we will see this personal connection with, "the Lord God liveth," He will demonstrate His power. Elijah did not have to go into a trance, or dance like the false priests for their dead god. He just had to call upon his God and this true and living God would respond.

BECAUSE HE LIVES

"As the Lord God liveth," means that Elijah would never be intimidated by the enormity of the challenge of the enemy. The way this is phrased is a direct testimony to the fact that I am able to do what I do because the Lord God liveth. The presence of enemies, the authority of enemies, the quantity of enemies cannot be compared even in the smallest way, to the Lord God of Israel that liveth. *"As the Lord God of Israel liveth,"* means that whatever happens on earth cannot affect the fact that the Lord God of Israel liveth. You know the old song that we sing, even today, *"Because He lives, I can face tomorrow, because He lives, all fear is gone."* This is really the testimony evident in the sudden emergence of Elijah. I am who I am, I was brought from where I was, because the Lord God of Israel liveth. Because

He did what he did for me, I have absolutely no doubt that He will continue doing what He is doing. *"As the Lord God of Israel liveth,"* carries a spiritual universe of glorious revelation. As Elijah had to deal with such astonishingly difficult, threatening challenges, only the true Lord God of Israel could empower him to function. He faced the challenge from the king, from Jezebel, from the false priests and prophets and from a rebellious Israel. These together formed a formidable overwhelming force but for the living Lord God, this was no challenge.

This Lord God of Israel that liveth is not only willing to touch, to deliver but He is able to deliver. All through Scripture there are celebrations of the fact that the Lord God liveth. There are hundreds of scriptures that speak of the glorious fact that the Lord liveth. To face seemingly insurmountable odds, to face these dire threats, to face possible death, Elijah had to know and to experience the fact that the Lord God of Israel liveth. He had the God-given ability to deal with all of this with such a force and passion. Nerves of steel, responses of power, and a life of demonstration, all because he knew and experienced, *"the Lord God of Israel liveth."*

THE LORD GOD

In saying very carefully and selecting the words, "The Lord God," Elijah displayed extremely important understanding in relation to the supremacy of God. By saying, *"Lord God,"* he was testifying to the sovereignty and the superiority of the living God. He is master and ruler and above Him there is no other. So it was not only the affirmation that He is the God that liveth, but that He is Lord God, the living God, and the sovereign God, the supreme God, the ruler of all. This is seen so gloriously all through Elijah's life. The Syrian army is blinded and captured, false prophets are killed, a widow's house becomes a supply house in famine, a son is raised, Ahab and Jezebel are defied. This is only to mention a few instances and there are many more where the sovereignty of God prevailed. All existing power and authority were effectively nullified as the Lord, the Master, the Sovereign began to move.

What an introduction to the ministry of this thunderous prophet! What an illustration of what can happen today because we serve the same God Who is the same yesterday, today and forever! Yes, our Lord God is sovereign and superior and no force that has been pitted against the Christian today can even compare on the smallest level to our Lord God. There should be no intimidation today by the forces that surround us, and no hesitation of God's people to take their positions. Elijah is known as the prophet of deeds and his life has become a pattern for all to follow. It so happens that this is the prophet that was chosen to have the most prolific future stretching straight into the time before the coming of the Lord. No adjectives can be too descriptive about this prophetic life and his mission. Yet to introduce it all and the foundation of it all was the Lord God of Israel and the Lord God of Israel who liveth. These are two foundational truths that are readily accessible to you right now. Our God is Lord, master, sovereign, supreme over-all and He is evermore alive.

Chapter 10

The First Man Standing

Verse one continues and says, *"Before whom I stand."* I am submitting to you that verse 1 becomes a pivotal, foundational verse for the future, dynamic demonstration throughout Elijah's life. In this verse he burst on the scene with heavenly thunder in his voice and goes straight to Ahab. His word to Ahab was not cordial or casual, it was not approving nor attesting, it was forceful, direct, unapologetic and conclusive. After this word, from verse two Elijah receives instructions from God that would take him on an amazing journey. Here, on this journey, we find a continuing prophetic pattern.

However in verse one, we see the emergence, the proclamation sent from heaven, the unafraid, unrelenting prophet and the pronouncement that would shut the heavens. Yes, verse one must be seen, experienced, understood and deeply internalized. He stood before the Lord. These words carry deep meaning, that are totally transforming. I stand before the Lord means that I acknowledge Him as the divine, ultimate authority. In this stand before Him I declare my submission to His authority. His stand before the Lord was an act of submission to the Lord. There are so many that fall so quickly in a time when the enemy comes against them. You may ask, *"With all the faith and word and teaching that they say they have, how are they so easily overcome by the slightest attack of the enemy?"*

I STAND SO I SUBMIT

It is impossible to stand before the majestic, magnificent Lord without the desire to willingly submit to Him. In that stand, with this submission to the divine authority, I am now authorized by Him. I can now exercise the authority to which I submit. My stand before God has authorized me to stand against the enemies that have come against me. All through the life of Elijah, we see no gimmicks, no weirdness, no indulgence into carnality. He stood, he submitted, he exercised authority and heaven responded and earth obeyed. As I stated earlier, the fight against the word submission has become monumental in the church. The lack of submission to divine authority is so visible and prevalent. We wonder why we do not see a greater demonstration of the authority of God through the people of the Lord. Could it be that because many have chosen not to submit to divine authority they cannot exercise divine authority? As I said before, you can only exercise authority to the extent to which you submit to authority.

Elijah's life was a visible demonstration of the authority of the Almighty God and we see where he was in total submission to God. If you stand for nothing, you will fall for anything. A stand before God, for God is required and it is not something that should be a request. What an honor it is to be given the privilege to stand before the Lord God Almighty, the creator of the universe, the supreme and sovereign God.

I STAND SO I AM OBEDIENT

To stand before the Lord God means that I am ready to be obedient and ready to do His bidding I am ready to be an instrument for the accomplishment of the divinely ordained task. As a result of the submission to His divine authority, my delight is to do His bidding. Doing His bidding now becomes a priority in my life so that I am free to become all I can be. Because of my Lord, my life now rushes to its fullest potential because I am now willing, in fact, it brings me great joy to do His bidding.

This I know, if He commands it, He will conquer it and He will fulfill it. Is this the time for the church to take its stand before the Lord? How can we have the power to stand against this present flood of evil, this avalanche of oppression without taking our stand before the Lord? This power, this authority comes from Him to me, then through me. There is no other place, no other person, that I can stand before and receive such a supernatural touch. Shall we allow, by silence and weakness, by the lack of response, this onslaught of evil to continue? Shall we remain immobilized and unmoved as our children and grandchildren suffer the consequences of renegade evil? Will the silence of the Christian continue so that this flood is uncontested? Who will take a stand before the Lord God and simultaneously take a stand against prevailing evils? May we fearlessly rebuke, stand against and repel these idolatrous attacks.

NO DEW – NO RAIN

Now we find out in the words Elijah spoke to Ahab and to the nation. The words that he uttered are the words that no nation, king or people want to hear. In the Middle East, one of the vital needs is the need for water. Because of the desert land, the people depend for life in the mountains and the valleys in the city and the country on WATER. When the streams and rivers are flowing, the pastures are green. No word could have presented more danger or devastation to a land than this word. No word could have attacked in judgment, a land that was filled with sin and idolatry as his word. *"There will be no dew or rain,"* these years upon you or your kingdom. Drought in this land.

This was a judgment from the palace to the prison, from the mountain to the valley from the rich to the poor. Ahab, your power is not important, your idols have no power, your lands will be scorched and the rivers will give no water. No one, regardless of position or power will be immune from this word. The green will be parched, the land will be thirsty and the population overrun with a judged land. Ahab, you have employed earthly things to bring abomination to this land but I stand before, I represent, I am the messenger of the Lord God of Israel. Heaven now speaks and your authority, your power, your queen mean nothing.

THE IDOLATRY OF TODAY

So here we are today in a place where secular humanism has tried to defy man and humanize God. They have tried to exalt law, medicine, philosophy above the knowledge of God. They have tried to wipe out any semblance of the true Lord God from the school system, from the courtrooms. Materialism, New Ageism, Agnosticism and many other 'isms' have tried to replace the Word of God. Some of these base elements have even entered the realm of some churches and scream from the pew and even from the pulpits. People in authority have tried to legalize things that the Bible teaches are immoral and devastating. What was at one time considered abominable evils have today been accepted and in some circles, preferred? The young generation has been trapped in this vortex of evil and they have no moral compass. From behavior, to dress, to relationships, no evil is out of bounds to many of the young gener-ation. Pornography has exploded and has become a profitable multibillion dollar business in America. Who will take a stand against this deception-de-cline, this immoral persuasion and this emotional landslide? Who will declare with power and author-ity, that there will be no rain, on these evils that prevail in our land? Who will call these people that uphold and expose these abominations into ac-countability? There are over 50 million babies that have been viciously killed in an abortion holocaust. Over 50% of marriages end up in divorce. Alcohol-ism and dope addiction have brought a part of soci-ety to the edge of disaster. Fatherless homes, children have no desire to submit to law. Who will rise today with a scorching word from God, and not be intimidated by what is around? The Lord God Almighty lives and it is before Him that I stand.

ACCORDING TO MY WORD

There will be no dew or rain these years accord-ing to my word. There are some powerful elements contained in these words. The King of Kings is speaking through Elijah to King Ahab. Heaven is about to shut off the rain from the earth. Eternity is about to interrupt time and there will be a period without rain. God's word is about to become Elijah's word so Elijah can say, according to my word. This is an astonishing exchange between heaven and earth but this is what the heart of God is all about. This is taught so prolifically in the New Testament — Matthew 6:10; Luke 12:32; Hebrews 6:4,5; 1 Corinthians 2:9,10; Colossians 1:12,13 state:

- Matthew 6:10 - *"Thy kingdom come, Thy will be done in earth, as it is in heaven.*
- Luke 12:32 - *Fear not, little flock; for it is your Father's good pleasure to give you the kingdom.*
- Hebrews 6:4,5 - [4] *For it is impossible for those who were once enlightened, and have tasted of the heavenly gift, and were made partakers of the Holy Ghost,* [5] *And have tasted the good word of God, and the powers of the world to come,*
- 1 Corinthians 2:9,10 - [9] *But as it is written, Eye hath not seen, nor ear heard, neither have entered into the heart of man, the things which God hath prepared for them that love him.* [10] *But God hath revealed them unto us by his Spirit: for the Spirit searcheth all things, yea, the deep things of God.*
- Colossians 1:12,13 - [12] *Giving thanks unto the Father, which hath made us meet to be*

partakers of the inheritance of the saints in light: [13] *Who hath delivered us from the power of darkness, and hath translated us into the kingdom of his dear Son.* "

There are many, many more in the New Testament but I quoted these to show you that the heart of God in the Old Testament and the New Testament is the same. His desire is to touch earth with Heaven, bring eternity into time, and show His Heavenly power in this earthly realm. What a loving, longsuffering, compassionate God we serve. This was a vivid story of Elijah. Life changed dramatically as this unusual, startling, dynamic prophet burst on the scene with thunderous power. Coming from his background as we previously explained, he did not show any bit of hesitation to speak, no timidity to stand and declare miraculous things. Not one residue of thought that said, well if this does not come to pass, I am a dead prophet. There is every evidence that he exuded the presence and the power of the Almighty God. Heaven-speaking, rain-stopping on an idolatrous kingdom, according to my word. All this sounds like the promise to the church of the New Testament. Remember, the Pastor in North Carolina who spoke to me. It is not only where is the God of Elijah, but where are the Elijahs of God? In the midst of the majority of Christians that are doing nothing but enjoying their blessings, there are a few, there is a remnant. These are the ones whom the Almighty God is seeking so that an entire region, an entire country, and an entire world can be impacted.

MY STAND MY WORD

He said all this is happening according to my word and later on he would gather the people around the altar to him. He used the words, *"according to my word."* This is either highly arrogant or this prophet understood something about identification which is a huge doctrine in the book of Romans.

The subject of identification is a wonderful teaching of Paul in the Book of Romans. Because of the love of God, I have been given a position from the Almighty God that should affect every area of my life. It is now my responsibility to identify with that position and those blessings. Because they have been given by God, all I do is to identify with that blessing and it becomes mine. Jesus died, so I died in Him. Jesus buried, so I was buried in Him. He rose again, so I rose in Him. These are all truths based on my position in Him and by identification. I walk in the power and reality of these truths.

I find Elijah displaying New Testament life in the Old Testament. How could this prophet that James says was, *"a man of like passions,"* say, *"According to my word."* It is because when you stand before the Lord, when all is submitted to the Lord, now you can speak for the Lord. You are now authorized to exercise the authority to which you have submitted. In this act of standing before and submitting to God, a dynamic infusion of God's power takes place. Now Elijah stands fearless before a mighty, yet human ruler. Ahab's wife is also a formidable enemy, yet human. They have behind them the power and authority of an empire, yet human. But here is Elijah, he stands before the King of Kings, who is divine. He has the power of the kingdom of Heaven behind him.

UNION WITH GOD

So when he stands before Ahab, Elijah is vitally connected and in complete union with the Glorious, Mighty God of Heaven. In the light of this union, this connection and with the infusion of this power, Ahab, Jezebel and their priests seem but a paltry few. Yes Ahab, I know who I was, where The Almighty God brought me from, and I know who I am today. I have taken my stand before the Lord God of Israel and now I take my stand against you.

So here is the today parallel. With all the evil, abomination, idolatry, the floods of oppressiveness that are present, where are the Elijahs of God? Sir, Madam, what word do you have in response to the presence of these enemies of God? What word do you have to give the ruling demonic forces that have affected your children and grandchildren, or your marriage, home and your life? Without the word of Elijahs, who will respond with aggressiveness, who will reprove these prevailing evils? Will we allow, by silence and fear, by apathy and indifference, these forces to continue unchecked? Is there a word from God in your heart? If so, rise up and deliver that word. The assaulting evils are myriad but the people with the Spirit of Elijah are here. There can be no avoiding this collision, this confrontation between the prevailing evils and those moving in the Spirit of Elijah. It is not only where is the God of Elijah, but also *"WHERE ARE THE ELIJAHS OF GOD?"*

Conclusion

1 Kings 17:2 says *"The word of the Lord came to Elijah saying."* After his stand against Ahab, God's word came giving him further direction. You can be assured when you are obedient to the call, the Almighty, will take you to higher places. Elijah was about to be taken on a powerful journey to experience a process that would produce a powerful product. He would be taken to Carmel where the ultimate showdown against the false prophets would take place.

In this process there are astonishing parallels to the life of the believer and many prophetic pictures of what the believer will face. This will be the subject of the next book on the Spirit of Elijah. As we bring this part of the revelation to an end, please understand that God is seeking His remnant saints. He will most likely find them in the oddest of places, some in the mountains surrounded by enemies, others in a desert, some hidden, others under great attack. But they all have one thing in common, they are ready to come out and are willing to be used in any way the Almighty chooses. It is a day of reckoning, it is a day when the move of God will call those who do not belong to the elite fleet, with no great pedigree or human credentials, it is the day when God will cause them to arise.

Never will our Lord allow the flood of evil to take charge of the world. There is a remnant, they may be few in comparison but Heaven's math is different and superior to human math. The one Abraham, the one Moses, the one Joshua, the one David, the one Solomon, the one Elijah, yes, the one carried the tide of human history to be turned by the power of God. So I declare that these are the days when a few, and it will become more, will begin flowing in the move of God. Here, the Ahabs will flee, the Jezebels will fall and become dog meat, the false priests will be rendered impotent. Yes, these are the days when the Spirit of Elijah is here. All the components for this confrontation are here. It is now battle time and we are present, accounted for and ready.

About Sherlock Bally

Sherlock Bally has been an ordained minister for thirty-five years. He attended Southern Bible College in Houston, Texas and did post graduate studies at Luther Rice Seminary and International Bible Seminary. After attending college, Sherlock went to Trinidad, where he was born, and pastored the church where he was saved. For fourteen years in Trinidad his duties included the pastorate of a growing church, a nationally televised program and a radio ministry reaching most of the Caribbean.

He was held hostage by fanatical Islamic adherents in 1990 and was miraculously delivered. His call to the nations led to a move back to the United States and from 1990 to 2007 he has made 62 overseas trips in crusades and conventions. He has appeared on the Trinity Broadcasting Network on several occasions, and makes several television and radio appearances. He has ministered with Hal Lindsey, Jack Van Impe, Grant Jeffrey, Perry Stone and many others. God has gifted Sherlock in the revelation of end-time prophecy and the subsequent application of prophetic truth to personal life. His passion is to see the lost saved, the saved sent and the sent empowered. He understands the primacy of the local church and the paramount position of the pastor in these days of harvest. He believes that this is the season of reclamation, restoration, and restitution.

Sherlock carries a powerful evangelistic anointing and thousands are saved in this country every year in his meetings. He is anointed to identify the attack of the enemy in everyday situations and arm believers with weapons of faith to win in the combat zone.

In 2006, Sherlock was appointed by the Christian Allies Caucus of the Knesset as their liaison to the pastors of North America. The Knesset is the government of Israel. The Christian Allies Caucus is comprised of fifteen members of Israel's government. Their purpose is to bring Israel and the Christians closer together. Sherlock sees this Judeo-Christian alliance as pivotal and an integral part and a vital component to Gods Timeline. Recently Dr. Bally was also named by the Christian Allies Caucus to be the Executive Director of the Caribbean Israel Allies Foundation. This foundation is dedicated to all the Islands of the Caribbean in order to bring all the people of the Caribbean in closer relationship to the Knesset.

He has authored over seven books and believes in the vital educational aspect of ministry. He is married to Renee' his wife of 32 years and is the father of Rachel and Micah.

Made in the USA
Columbia, SC
15 July 2019